MW01601600

THE NEW DREAM BOOK

A COMPLETE FORTUNE TELLER

First Edition 1816
Richard Scott

New Edition 2018
Edited by Tarl Warwick

COPYRIGHT AND DISCLAIMER

FOREWORD

This following work is one of various interesting texts of divination I have encountered in my time editing manuscripts of occultism: This general tradition encompasses several distinct traditions which, from the mid 18th century to the early 20th, intertwined at times; works that often heavily borrowed one anothers' ideas and in some cases explicitly ripped one another off, borrowing, sometimes verbatim, entire passages and sections.

As this work dates to 1816, it is obviously one of the earlier variants of fortune telling lore in this tradition; we can roughly classify the tradition into four separate strands; the oracle tradition (most famously within "Napoleon's Oraculum"- a very nice work I have edited), the dream book (as the present text is), the folk prognosticator (sort of almanac style lore, such as fortune telling by moles, lines on the hand, or tea leaves), and finally the semi-modern fortune telling practices such as card throwing or using dice. The number of works within this tradition is rather large and it's a fairly good bet that there are works of this general sort, encompassing one or more of these subjects, that were either self released or released in small enough batches to now be extinct, virtually or literally, as texts at all; forgotten works, of which a copy or two might exist, at most, in some attic sealed up for the last half century.

This present work has one of the better, more expansive sections on interpreting dreams, which makes sense, considering its actual title. We then have to consider another tenet of this practice as held prior to the roughly late pre-modern era (the forties and fifties) as opposed to the truly modern era (subjectively speaking at the time of this writing of course.) Fortune teller works were always meant to appeal to a broad audience of largely poor and middle class lay people; while upper society would have purchased such works, that alone was a sliver of the population, and when you still only get the two shillings for a work sold whether the person you sold it to is rich or poor, it favors a work that appeals to a much broader collective; in the early 19th century, that meant farmers, laborers, tradesmen, and housewives, which encompassed most of the population in generally literate Western Europe and the early, burgeoning United States.

Therefore those used to dream interpretation which answers psychological or spiritual things (as they tend to today) may be confused as to why most of the fixation in this and other pre-20th century works of the kind revolves around finding a marital partner, courting, planting crops, and conducting trade by land and sea. Imprisonment is also a common topic, as well as friendships, that is, in physical proximity. Today, dreams are used less to predict and more to reflect, upon the current and past, and the psychology of the dreamer. In my own humble opinion, these older works more closely reflect the true human condition, since it bereaves it of several massive layers of psychological artifice.

This edition of the New Dream Book has been carefully edited for grammer and word usage, and has been modernized where it is possible to do so without altering the meaning. Care has been taken to avoid the same and to preserve the document.

THE COMPLETE DREAM BOOK

We shall begin this work with the explanation of dreams, which have always a reference to some transaction that is about to take place; for if a man was narrowly to watch his dreams, he would find that he was always forewarned of the occurrence about to happen in those moments, when both the body and mind seem lost m the soft slumbers of oblivion. For the sake of enabling our readers more readily lo refer to them, we have arranged them alphabetically.

ONEIROLOGY

Or, the science of foretelling future events by dreams

ABUSE: To dream that you are abused and insulted, is a certain sign that some dispute will happen between you and some person with whom you have business; therefore, after such a dream, you should be particularly careful of yourself and be as gentle and mild as possible, that you may not give those with whom you have dealings any advantage over you- if you are in love, be assured that some one has attempted to injure you with the object of your affection, and that they have in a great measure succeeded you should, therefore, after such a dream, be particularly complaisant and attentive; by this means you will eradicate the unfavorable impressions that have been made against you- if you have a law-suit, keep a sharp look out alter your attorney, for such a dream in that case denotes, that he is endeavoring to sell your cause- avoid, after such a dream, taking a journey by land, or a voyage by sea, for eight and forty hours, because such a dream forebodes accidents by traveling.

ADULTERY: To dream of the commission of this sin, forebodes great troubles and misfortunes; if you are in love, you will certainly fail in marrying the object of your wishes. If you have a law-suit, it will certainly go against you, by the treachery of those who pretend to be your friends. If you are in business some heavy loss will happen to you. Such a dream announces that you are in great danger of losing your liberty, and if you are about to take a voyage by sea, omit it for the present, for you will never reach the destined port. To dream you were tempted to commit this crime, and that you resisted it, is an happy omen-everything will flourish with you- be sure it is a good time to begin trade after such a dream. If you have a law-suit all will go in your favor, with credit to yourself and confusion to your opponents- if you are about to take a long journey, it will be pleasant and successful to your object. If you are going to sea, you will have an agreeable voyage, fine weather, and a quick arrival at the port of destination. If you are in love, press the object of your wishes for they will be gratified.

ABEL: To dream of this second son of Adam, the victim of his brother's vengeance and jealousy, and the first man that stained the earth with his blood, is a favorable omen, portends future elevation and grandeur. If you have law-suit, it will terminate in your favor. If you are in love, the mistress of your heart will be kind and faithful. If you are about to commence trade, your business will thrive, and you will become rich. If you are a farmer, be sure of good crops the ensuing season. If you are about to undertake a journey, it will be prosperous to you; in short, expect to rise to honors, dignity, and affluence. Observe one thing, that should he speak to you in your dream, you should be very careful to mind what he says, as otherwise you may mar all your good fortune, and reverse every benefit that fortune has in store for you.

ABRAHAM: To dream of this patriarch is favorable to the person who dreams. It in general denotes accumulation of riches and of honors; in a woman, it denotes, that she will have many children; if you are in love, it denotes you will have many rivals; if you have a law-suit, it. forebodes that many difficulties will occur. If you are in business, then it portends a great increase of your business, and that you will employ many hands to conduct it. You must also be very observant of what he says to you, for he will perhaps inform you how to avoid some misfortune, or how to attain to riches and honors.

ADAM: To dream you see this father of man, this inhabitant of Paradise, who was betrayed by Eve into sin, is an happy omen; if he looks pleasant be sure you will succeed in whatever you undertake. If you are in love, expect your mistress to smile on your love, and to reward your constancy. If you have a law-suit, expect it to be given much in your favor by the judge. If you are a farmer, expect an abundant crop, and that your pigs, poultry, and cattle, will increase very fast, and be of a good kind, and fetch the best price at market. If you are about to quit your native place, abandon the idea, for depend some benefit is in store for you in the place where you had birth. If you have already quit it, I would advise you, if you can, to return, for there lies your fortune and prosperity; do not undertake travel unless absolutely necessary, for although they will be successful, yet you will still be more fortunate by resting at home. If he looks displeased and angry, then you must use great caution in all your dealings, for some mischief is intended you, but you will get the better of it, but on no account undertake a voyage by sea, neither borrow nor lend money, for at least a month or two, because, if you do, you will lose what you lend and what you borrow will bring you into trouble; be careful, if he speaks to you, to mind what he says, and observe it as faithfully as you possibly can.

ADVERSARY: To dream you meet with an adversary denotes that you will overcome some obstacle to your happiness. If you are a lover, you will conquer some powerful rival, and be happy in your love; it also denotes, that your affairs are going on well. If you arc soliciting a place, it portends you are about to get it and if you are in trade, it forebodes some good orders, and an increase of business. If you quarrel, and he overcomes you, it is a good sign, for you will conquer all obstacles to your promotion, happiness, and fortune; but if you conquer him, then it denotes that you will never rise to any great preferment by the means you are at present adopting, that many things will miscarry with you, but in general you will be fortunate. Should he draw blood of you, you will surely lose your liberty for a time, but will afterwards be flourishing and happy.

AQUAINTANCE: To dream you quarrel or fight with an acquaintance is an unlucky omen; it forebodes a division among your own family, much to the injury and prejudice of the dreamer. If you are in love, your mistress will prove unfaithful, and marry some other man that she has told you she most hates. If you are in business, some heavy loss will befall you; you will disagree with some of your best friends on the most trivial matters, which will end in an open rupture; if you are a farmer, expect a bad crop, the murrain among your cattle, that your pigs and poultry will fail, and not fetch good prices. If you have a law-suit, depend, that your attorney will neglect you, that your witnesses will be tardy and backward, and that finally you will lose your cause. Do not for some time undertake a journey by land, or a voyage by sea, and enter for the present into no new undertaking, for you will be unsuccessful. Quit, if you can, your present place of residence, and above all, avoid lending money, for you will surely lose it, together with the friendship of those to whom you lend it.

AGUE: To dream you have an ague, denotes nothing very particular, more than you are in danger of becoming a drunkard and a glutton. If you have any relation or friend that h ill, it denotes they will recover. And if you have a law-suit, that it will be settled in your favor. If you are in love, it forewarns you, that if you do not immediately marry you will lose your mistress. If you dream another has an ague, then it denotes a variety of fortune, that you will sometimes be rich, and sometimes poor; that you trill have much trouble, lose your liberty, and die before you are fifty. To dream your sweetheart has an ague, is a lucky omen, it shews you are beloved, and that you w ill be happy with the object of your wishes, but never very rich.

AIR: To dream of the atmosphere, has a variety of interpretations, and depends entirely on the different appearances it has. If you dream the sky is clear, of a fine blue, calm and serene, then it is a good omen; you will be successful in your enterprises. If you are soliciting any place or preferment, you will surely obtain it- if you are in love, you will surely marry the object of your affections. Have you a law-suit? You will gain it- are you in trade? it will flourish and be profitable- are you a farmer? good crops will attend you, your cattle will increase, your pigs and poultry will be abundant, your commodities will fetch a good price at market; are you married? You will have many children, and they will be dutiful and do well. Are you about to undertake a journey? it will answer your utmost expectations; are you going to sea? you will have a pleasant and prosperous voyage; are you in debt? you will speedily be enabled to extricate yourself from it; are you imprisoned? you will shortly be set at liberty; are you going into business? you will succeed, and have many friends; are you in poverty? riches will quickly drive away its remembrance; have you a quarrel? it will soon be made up to your advantage; in short, whatever point you aim at, it will be crowned with success.

To dream it is streaked with white, denotes that many severe difficulties will befall you, over which you will eventually triumph; you will perhaps go to jail, but you will come out again shortly with honor and credit to yourself; it forebodes that many enemies will attack you both openly and secretly, that they will appear to have the advantage over you for a time, but in the end they will be routed and overcome by you. Your children will get into troubles, out of which you will extricate them; if you are in love, many crosses will happen to you, and for a time you will appear to lose the affections of your sweetheart, but in the end you will marry and be happy, and have fin€ children; if you have a law-suit, you will have much trouble and vexation, but you will gain it after all. If you are in business, many difficulties will occur, which friends will remove, and you will at last be prosperous; if you go to sea, you w ill be cast away, but get safe ashore, and be favorably received by the inhabitants of the country. If you borrow money, you will be much slandered and abused by the person who lends it to you; if you lend money, you will have great trouble in recovering it. It portends, that you will have a light illness, but your health, will be much better afterwards.

To dream that it is full of thick, dark, and heavy clouds, is an unfavorable token; you will fall sick and perhaps die; disappointments will attend your business. If you are in love, you will not marry the person you intended; if you have a law-suit you will lose it; if you go to sea you will have bad weather, meet with storms and shipwreck, and lose all your, property; you will lose some friend, or near relation by death; many friends will desert you; you will grow melancholy, and every thing will cross your expectations; therefore, after such a dream you should change your situation, be what it may.

To dream that the sky is streaked with red, and looks fiery, denotes, that in love you will be successful, in business not so; it also forewarns you that some friend or relation will be killed in battle, and that sickness will attend your family; if you have a son he will get into many difficulties, and narrowly escape losing his life; a journey by land will injure your health and pocket, but a voyage by sea will be prosperous, and conducive to your health. If you are in prison, you will remain there sometime. If you owe any money, I advise you to pay it immediately, otherwise it will bring you into trouble. Whatever you lend you will lose, but if you have any hopes of getting a place, you will, after some trouble, succeed, and it will turn out lucrative. It also denotes that the next woman you meet, not of your own family, will be your enemy and endeavor to cause you injury. This you may prevent by being very civil and obliging to her, which will allay her resentments against you. If you are a farmer you will have but indifferent crops, and will lose some of your horses by sickness or accident. If your father and you are at variance, depend it will be speedily made up, and that he will befriend you; but be very cautious of quarreling, for you will have the worst of it. You will get some small matter by legacy, but it will not do you much good.

ALTAR: To dream you are at the altar and receiving the holy sacrament, is a very unfavorable omen and denotes many heavy and severe afflictions, and that you will be very unsuccessful in your pursuits, and have much trouble in overcoming your difficulties. If you are in love, your sweetheart will die before you marry, or else be removed very far from you forever. If you are in business, heavy losses will attend you, and you will with great difficulty keep from going to prison, you will lose many friends by death, sickness will come upon you and your family, and your children will be undutiful and turn out bad.

ANCHOR: To dream of this emblem of hope, denotes some good to the dreamer; it forebodes many unexpected successes. If you are in love, it warns you to be assiduous and attentive to obtain the object of your wishes, otherwise your passion will not meet with success. If you are in trade, then it forebodes success at a distant period, after you had nearly given over all expectation of doing well; expect shortly to see some friend who has been at sea, and that he has escaped some perilous situation. It forebodes, that lawsuits will attend you, in which you will not gain much, although you will not be much injured by them. Beware of some friend who pretends you more than ordinary attachment, he will deceive you, and endeavor though vainly to harm you. You will have many children, chiefly girls, and the third born will be the best off in this world.

ANGELS: To dream you see angels in your sleep is a sure sign that some one is near you. Therefore be mindful of the rest of your dream, for it will come to pass pretty accurately; should you only dream you see nothing but an angel, or angels, then it denotes health, prosperity, and much happiness, with many children, who will all turn out good. If a woman with child dreams of them, she will have a good time and perhaps twins. If you are in love, nothing can be more favorable, and all your undertakings will prosper, and be advantageous to you,

ANGER: To dream that you are in a passion and angry with any one, denotes you have many enemies, and that some evil design is formed against your happiness and security. If you are in love, be sure that some dangerous rival is slandering you to your sweetheart. If you are at law with any one, depend that secret attempts are making to sell your cause; if you are in business look carefully after your servants, for you are forewarned that they are about to plunder you, and do you an injury; be careful whom you trust, for some swindler will attempt to defraud you, and without great care on your part will be successful. If you are going a journey, avoid traveling by night or alone in bye places; for such a dream denotes, you will be robbed and ill treated. If you dream you see another in a passion with you, it is rather more favorable, but still forebodes some very unpleasant misfortunes about to happen to you; if you are in love, your sweetheart will fall sick and experience some heavy loss. If you are in business some creditors will become very troublesome to you, and perhaps arrest you; if you have a lawsuit, you will find great difficulty in getting money to carry it on; if you are going to sea, storms will arise, and you will have a very dangerous passage; if you journey by land, you will fall sick on the road and be unsuccessful in what you are about.

ANTS: To dream of these industrious little insects, has a variety of interpretations, and depends upon the manner in which you dream of them. If you see them running about, it denotes that you will be a great loser by some plan that you will undertake for gain, and that you will be considerably the sufferer by an avaricious disposition. If you are in love, too great a regard to the dower of your intended wife will break off the match; if you are going to sea with merchandise you will be taken in when you most expect to make a good bargain. If you have a lawsuit, you will lose it, although circumstances may appear much in your favor. In short, some speculation by which you expect to make much money, will go very near to ruin you. If you dream you see them busily employed laying in their winter stores, it is a good omen- things will prosper with you; if you undertake a journey, it will turn out well; if you are in love, your love will be crowned with success, and if you are in business, your affairs mil prosper and you will grow rich, get many friends, and arrive at considerable honors in the state. If you are a farmer, plentiful crops of corn will gild your fields, your hay harvest will be abundant, your cattle will multiply, your sows will have large litters, your hens will hatch many chickens, your poultry in general will increase very fast and your commodities will fetch the best price at market. If you go to sea, you will get money by it; if you are married, you will have an affectionate wife and many children, with ample means of supporting them; in short, your concerns will prosper, and you will be very happy. If they appear to be devoured by other animals, and otherwise injured and trodden upon, then it is a bad omen; secret enemies are compassing your ruin; some bosom friend will deceive you; your sweetheart will be unkind and perhaps unfaithful; your business will be unproductive, bad crops will attend your cultivation, and your commodities will not fetch a good price at market. If you go to sea, misfortunes will attend your voyage; if you have a lawsuit, you will surely lose it by the perfidy of some pretended friend; if you journey by land, you will be attacked by robbers, and robbed of whatever you have.

If they are entirely destroyed, you will get into prison, your business will fail. If you are in love, your sweetheart will not reward your passion; if you are a farmer, your cattle will die of the murrain, and your crop. He unproductive; if you go to sea, you will be cast away and lose your all; if you expect a place you will be disappointed; and if you are in a good place you will lose it; sickness will attack you, your thread of life will be cut shorty your children will die, and your wife become unfaithful. In short, the most dismal reverse will happen to you, and disaster attend all your attempts. If you dream of these insects when you are sick, you must expect to recover very slowly, and to be a long time before you are able to work.

APES: To dream of these mischievous animals, forebodes no good; they are a certain sign of wicked and secret enemies, who will seek by many devices to injure you, be therefore upon your guard, for some one who pretends to be your friend, is about to deceive you, and you are very near losing your liberty; after such a dream a change of place is advisable; if you are in love, do not attempt to marry your then sweetheart, for he or she will prove unfaithful, and involve you in much trouble. If you have a lawsuit with anyone, make it up as soon as you can, otherwise it will injure you greatly. If you are in business, be extremely circumspect in your transactions, for danger is near; you will lose some friends by the malicious persecution of a pretended friend of your own.

APPAREL: Nothing more demonstrates the events that

are about to happen to you, than dreaming of wearing apparel; but almost every color has a different interpretation, and must depend on its appearing new or old, its fitting you, or being too big or too little. We shall here explain them according to their different significations.

To dream you are dressed m white, is a sure token of success in the first object you undertake, and that you will be successful in love, and that your sweetheart is of good temper and amiable disposition.

To dream you are dressed in green denotes that you are about to take a journey to your advantage, and that your sweetheart prefers you to all other lovers.

To dream you are dressed in black is an unlucky omen; some quarrel is about happen between you and a friend or a relation; sickness is about to attend you raid your family; death will deprive you of some near friend or relation; lawsuits will perplex and harass you; if you undertake a journey, it will be unsuccessful, and contribute much to injure your health and fortune. If you are in love, it denotes that your sweetheart is very unhappy and that sickness will attend her. If you are a farmer, you will be cheated by some knave, and your crops will turn out indifferent, the murrain will attack your cattle, and some dreadful accident will happen by the overturning of one of your wagons. If you are in business, some one will arrest you, and you will have great difficulty in settling the matter.

To dream you are dressed in blue denotes happiness; you will shortly be invited to some banquet or merrymaking, when you will make some friends and be very happy, if you only avoid quarreling, to which some enemy to your welfare will excite you. Your sweetheart is by this color denoted to be very faithful to you, and will make you very happy and comfortable. You will have many children chiefly boys, who w ill turn out honest and good ; if you are in trade you will prosper.

If you dream you are dressed in scarlet, you are thereby warned of some very heavy calamity, and a severe fit of illness; your sweetheart is by it announced to you to be of a turbulent disposition, much inclined to dispute about trifles, and liable to make you very unhappy; your children will be but short lived and of very unhappy tempers much inclined lo be very sickly; it surely denotes a quarrel and the loss of friends.

To dream you are dressed in yellow, is rather lucky than otherwise, but your sweetheart by it appears to be very jealous of you, and great pains will be requisite to prevent your separating; if you are married, keep a good lookout, for someone is about to alienate the affections of your partner. In trade, it promises prosperity, but someone will cheat you out of a trifle not of much consequence. If you are a farmer, you will have an abundant crop; if you undertake a voyage by sea, you will be greatly the gainer by it; and if you expect any place or preferment, after much trouble you will attain it.

To dream you are dressed in crimson denotes that the dreamer will live to a good old age, and be neither very fortunate or unfortunate through life; you are about to experience some very pleasant news from a distant quarter, and from those you thought dead; your sweetheart will be obliged to leave you for a time, but will continue faithful to you. If you are in trade you will experience some loss by a person you had great confidence in, but you will nearly at the same time, get a job that will amply make you amends; it denotes a small dispute between a landlord and his tenant, which will be settled amicably to the advantage of the latter.

To dream you are dressed in a variety of colors, denotes

a variety of fortunes is about to attend you. Old friends will desert you, new ones will supply their place; if you are in love, a quarrel will take place between you and your sweetheart, which will, after much uneasiness to both parties, be adjusted by friends; be cautious in what you do for some lime, for many traps will be laid to ensnare you, but on no account trust yourself on the water; your relations will shortly die, and if you have any children, sickness will attend them . If you are sick at the time of the dream, it denotes a happy and speedy recovery.

To dream you are fashionably dressed, and in good company, is very good for the dreamer; he will rise considerably above his present condition. Your sweetheart will prefer you above others, and be very good tempered; whatever you undertake will have a prosperous issue, and some unexpected news of an agreeable nature will reach you. Expect to see a long absent friend return in very good circumstances; but avoid having a dispute with any one, for it will go against you and do much harm, particularly if it be with your sweetheart.

To dream you are dressed shabbily, that your clothes are gouged and torn, is a very bad omen. If you are in love, it denotes you will never marry the person to whom you are attached; some heavy and afflicting loss is about to attend you; you will surely go to jail, unless you take extraordinary care; if you are married, you will quarrel with your spouse, and much domestic strife will ensue. If you go to sea, you will be cast away, and in great danger of starving. If you are in business, you will be robbed of a considerable quantity of goods; and the next parcel of goods you purchase you will lose by; if you are a farmer, beware what company you keep when you go to market, for sharpers will lay wait for you, and endeavor to cheat you. If it is hay time, look well to your hay ricks, for such a dream denotes that a rick will take fire, and be burnt to rubbish. Some quarrel will ensue between you and a friend, which will end to your disadvantage.

To dream your clothes fit you well, and are comfortable to the season of the year, is favorable and denotes success. If you are in love, you will be speedily married- if you are married you will soon have a child, most likely a boy, if it is, he will be a great scholar, and be advanced to great dignities in the state.

To dream your clothes do not fit you, and that they are not suitable to the season, denotes the death of some friend, and a loss by fire. If you are in love, the person who is your lover is not the one intended to marry you. It also denotes the place you live in is not calculated for your prosperity and happiness, and is a warning for you to quit it. If you have children, some one of them will shortly be in great affliction; if they are grown up, one of them is near losing its liberty; if they are young, then expect sickness to afflict one of them severely.

To dream you see another dressed in any of the modes above described, forebodes to the person dreamed of, the same fortunes, and in a much smaller degree, the same events to yourself.

To dream you are dressed in new clothes, is a very favorable omen, it portends honors and success to your undertakings. You may expect also to see some long absent friend, and to receive a small legacy, or some debt which you had given up. It is a most certain prognostic of marriage, and portends a very favorable reception with your lover. If you journey by land or by sea, it will be pleasant and profitable. It forebodes many children, who will make you happy; and if you have quarreled with any one, it warns you that you should now attempt to make up the breach, because the parties are favorably inclined towards you.

NEW DREAM BOOK

APPARITION: To dream you see a ghost, hobgoblin, specter, and such kind of things, is of a very unfortunate nature, they denote vexation and disappointment. If you are in love, it is a certain sign of your not being beloved in turn, that the object of your affections either hates you or despises you. Depend upon it some one is about to deceive yon, and that you are in the habits of friendship with one who is your most inveterate enemy. Do not undertake a journey just at the time, for it will be unfortunate to you, and be careful of contracting debts, for such a dream forebodes great trouble through some one to whom you shall owe money.

ARMS: To dream your arms are withered, is a certain sign that you will decay in health and fortune. To dream they are growing strong, signifies that some expected success will attend you; and if you have a brother who has children, his eldest child will be the means of augmenting your prosperity, and averting from you some dreadful evil. It signifies success in love, and that your sweetheart is faithful. Riches will attend you and some unpleasant quarrels will be made up to your advantage.

To dream your arms are broken, denotes the loss of some near friend or relation. It is a bad prognostic, and denotes looses in trade, and if you are in love, your sweetheart will be removed to a great distance from you, and perhaps marry another without great caution on your part. To dream your right arm is cut off, denotes you will lose some near male relation.

To dream your left is cut off, denotes you will lose some near female relative. For a married woman to dream her arms have grown lusty and strong, denotes that she will have many male children, that her husband will arrive at public honors, and will grow rich, and make many friends.

ASPS: To dream of asps, denotes that you will become

extremely rich, and have great quantities of money by you; if you are in love, it imports that your love will be returned, and that your sweetheart will become through your means extremely wealthy.

ASSES: To dream you see jack-asses is a good sign. If you have servants they will be faithful and diligent, if you are in love, your sweetheart will be kind and true, if you are in trade, your business will flourish, if you are a farmer, you will have good crops, and thrive well in your present farm, if you are going a journey by land or water, it will prove pleasant and successful.

To dream you are riding on an ass, it is the forerunner of some foolish quarrel, in which you will be much in the wrong, and condemned by your friends, if you are in love, it denotes that some misunderstanding will happen between you and your sweetheart in which you will be much in fault, if you are in business, it foretells that you will make some foolish bargain.

To dream you are driving an ass, denotes that you will fail into some trouble, of which you will get the better and that you will be relieved from present embarrassments; if you are in love, it denotes that some quarrel will take place between your sweetheart and yourself, which will soon be made up again to your advantage.

To dream an ass runs after you, denotes that some slander will be raised against you by some foolish persons, who will become themselves the victims of the scandal raised against you. To dream you see an ass fully loaded, is of very good import, and shews that yon will be the founder of your own fortune, which will be considerable. If you are in love, it warns you that some wealthy person is about to estrange the affections of your sweetheart. If you are in business, it foretells great success and plenty of trade. If you are a married woman, it denotes that you will have a son, who will by his own industry, attain great riches, and rise to high honors in the state. If you are a farmer, you will have an abundant crop, and a great increase in your cattle and poultry. It also denotes that some near relation will make a great fortune in foreign parts, which he will bring over with him, and spend in his native place.

BACK: To dream you show your naked back, is a certain sign that you will be engaged in some lewd action, and that your sweetheart will prove false to you, it forebodes loss by traveling, and that your friends are fickle and unsteady. To dream of the back bone, is a lucky omen, it demotes health and prosperity in your undertakings. If you are in love, your sweetheart will be faithful, and you are very near marrying. It also denotes that you will have many children, and be very happy- if you are in business, it forebodes great success in trade, and some good orders by which you will be a considerable gainer. To dream that your back has broke out in sores and blotches, denotes that you will be injured by some secret enemies. If you are in love, it signifies to you that your sweetheart is about to prefer some rival whom you know not of. To dream you have broken your back foretells misfortunes; expect some very heavy loss, either of money or friends. If you are in love, it forebodes the death of your sweetheart, and to a farmer it foretells bad crops, with some severe loss among his cattle. To dream you are grown strong in your back, denotes that some legacy will fall to you, and that you will unexpectedly become rich. If you are in love, you will shortly marry the object of your affections, and have many children. To a man, it denotes that he will shortly see the woman who is to be his wife, and to a woman, that she will soon see the man destined to be her husband, and that they will become rich, and be very happy.

BAILIFFS: To dream you are arrested by bailiffs, is a sign that you will escape some heavy misfortune; but it also foretells, that your present sweetheart will never marry you, and that you will be overreached in a bargain.

BEARD: For a man to dream he has a long beard, denotes good fortune. If he is in trade, be will thrive; if he is in love be will marry the present object of his affections, who will bring him some money; if he is a farmer, it denotes good crops, and an addition to his farm. If a married woman dreams of a beard, it is unlucky, it foretells the loss of her husband, and that she will fall into great distress. If a maid dreams of a beard, it denotes that she will be quickly married, and that her first and second child will be boys. If a woman with child dreams of a beard, it is a sign of a good labor, and that the fruit in her womb is a boy. For a woman to dream that she has a beard, is a very lucky omen, and denotes that she will speedily attain her most sanguine desires.

BACON: To dream of bacon, denotes the death of some friend or relation, and that enemies will endeavor to do you a mischief; in love, it denotes disappointment and discontent.

BAGPIPES: To dream of this instrument of Scottish music, indicates, that the dreamer will experience great trouble, and that he will labor hard to little purpose; in love, it denotes that the marriage state will be full of cares, and that you will in it experience much poverty and distress; it also denotes bad success at sea, and forebodes shipwreck, and a narrow escape from death.

BARN: To dream of a barn,, and that you see it well stored with corn, denotes much good; if you have a dispute, you will gain the advantage over your adversary; if you are in trade, you will flourish, and grow rich, and have good servants if you employ none under the age of sixteen; you may expect to have a legacy of land; it foretells to a man that he will marry some rich woman; to a maid that she will marry a man who will grow very rich by his industry, and be promoted in the state. If you are in love, it denotes that your sweetheart is true, and will marry you; that you will have many children, who will all become rich, and that the husband will die first leaving his widow extremely well of in the world. If you dream you see an empty barn, the reverse will happen.

BASIN: To dream you are eating or drinking out of a basin is a certain sign that you will soon be in love, but without great care you will not marry the first object of your affections; it denotes prosperity in trade and to the farmer. If you are a seafaring man, it indicates that at the next port you touch at you will fall in love.

BATHING.: To dream of a bath is a very unpropitious omen; expect after it to experience many hardships and much sorrow; if you are in love, your sweetheart will experience many crosses and losses. But to dream you are bathing yourself in clear water, denotes happiness, prosperity, and success in love; if the water is dirty, then it foretells shame and sorrow, and a disappointment in love.

BAY TREE: To dream of a bay tree, denotes success in your undertakings, and that you will marry a rich person; if you are going to sea, it is a very favorable omen; if your lover be at sea, expert he will soon return in a much wealthier condition than he left you.

BEANS: To dream of beans is an unfavorable dream. It is the forerunner of troubles and quarrels; if you are in love, expect a difference to happen between you and your sweetheart.

BEAR: To dream of a bear is not a good omen; expect to have much vexation and that some powerful enemy will attempt lo do you an injury- if you are in love, some richer person will estrange the love of your sweetheart, but they will never be happy. If you are soliciting a place, depend you will lose it by some person of more interest stepping in between you and your patron.

BEES: To dream of these little industrious insects, who collect the sweets of every flower, have a variety of interpretations according to their different situations. To dream they sting you, denotes loss of good character; and if you are in love of your sweetheart.

To dream you see them at work, is a very lucky dream, it forebodes great success by your own industry; if you are a farmer, be sure of good crops; if you are in love, be sure you will marry the object of your affections and that you will have many children and become rich. To dream you see them making their honey under your own roof, is the best omen in the world, be sure that it denotes dignity in the state, riches, a good husband or wife, and many good children, in short, that whatever you take in hand will be prosperous; if you are soliciting a place, depend you will gain it and afterwards be promoted. For the rich to dream of bees is rather unlucky; but to the poor, they denote comfort, affluence, and success.

BEGGARS: To dream of beggars, is rather unfavorable especially to lovers, and persons in business. To dream they beg alms of you, and that you refuse it, denotes misery, want, and a prison; if you are in love, some scandalous person will ruin it with your sweetheart. To dream that you give them alms, indicates success in business and that you will obtain after much difficulty the object of your affections; your children will be sickly and narrowly escape many dangers.

BED: To dream you go to the bedside of your lover,

foretells a speedy marriage; if you dream you go between the sheets, you will have a child within twelve months after marriage, who will become rich, and afford you support in your old age.

BEHEADING: To dream you see anyone beheaded, is a good omen; if you are in love, you will marry the object of your affections ; if you are in prison you will speedily gain your liberty; if you are in trouble of any kind, it will speedily vanish; it denotes also that you will see some friend who has long been absent, and that he will be in good health.

BELLS: To dream you hear the bells ringing, denotes a speedy marriage, and that you will receive some outcry of good news.

BIRDS: To dream of these feathered inhabitants of the air, is indicative of various fortune. To dream you hear them singing is a favorable omen; expect to have much joy; if you are a married man and have children, something will happen greatly to the advantage of your family; if you are in love your sweetheart much wishes for the marriage and will make you very happy. If you are in business, success will attend you.

To dream you see them flying denotes that you are about to undertake a long voyage by sea; if they appear to fly swiftly and are sportive, your voyage will be prosperous and pleasant, but if they appear to fly slowly, expect much sickness and shipwreck.

To dream of finding a bird's nest, if it has eggs in it, is a very lucky dream, but much better if it has young ones. To dream of a bird's nest, and that it is empty, foretells much disappointment and uneasiness- expect to be imprisoned, for it forebodes loss of liberty. If you dream you see a great number of birds assembled together, you will be present at some trial.

BLEEDING: To dream you are bleeding, denotes loss of goods and character, and that your sweetheart will not marry you. To dream you see another bleeding, indicates that some person who pretends to be your friend is about to take some great advantage of you. To dream you draw blood of another, denotes that you will recover a lawsuit, and be successful in love and in business. To dream another draws blood of you, is a certain prognostic that you will be unsuccessful in love and in business and every thing you undertake.

BLIND: To dream of being blind is a certain sign that you repose your confidence in some person who is your bitter enemy; it denotes also, that your sweetheart is unfaithful, and prefers another. In business, it denotes that you will lose money, and that your servants want fidelity.

BLOWING THE FIRE: To dream you are blowing the fire, indicates to the lover, that your sweetheart is very angry with you- to the poor man, it denotes riches and success in life; to the rich man it foretells poverty and disappointment. If a master has such a dream, it signifies that he will become a servant, if a servant dreams of it, it denotes that he will become a master.

BOAR: To dream of a boar, denotes to the lover that some rival will attack your sweetheart, and you will be in great danger of losing the object of your affections. If you are a farmer, it denotes that heavy rains and a tempest will damage your corn. If you are in trade some one will oppose you among your connections; it also denotes that you will speedily have a quarrel with some person. If the boar is running, you will have the advantage, if not your adversary will triumph over you.

NEW DREAM BOOK

BOAT: To dream that you are on the water in a boat provided you are in company, denotes prosperity and success in your undertakings; if you are in love, your sweetheart will be faithful and will marry you, and if the water throws up little bubbles, you will have many children, chiefly girls; it also signifies that the dreamer will speedily be at a wedding. If you dream you are in a boat alone it is a bad omen; to the lover, it denotes the loss of your sweetheart, who will prefer another; it also denotes that you will be forsaken by your friends, and that your undertakings in life will be unsuccessful. To dream the boat capsizes, is the most fatal omen in the world; let your expectations be what they may, renounce them for they will never be fulfilled. If you are soliciting a place, depend you will never get it if you are in love, depend you will never marry the object of your affections.

BREWING AND BAKING: To dream you are occupied in any of these matters denotes that your servants are very idle, and that you are in danger of being much injured by them. If you are in love, it denotes that your sweetheart is of an idle disposition, and that you will become poor by marriage with the present object of your afections.

BREAD: To dream of bread, is in general a favorable omen. To dream you see a great quantity of loaves, denotes success in life; if you are in love, it imports that your lover is of an industrious turn, that you will marry the object of your affections, and will be very happy, become rich, and have many children. To dream you are eating good bread, denotes that you will be shortly married. To dream the bread is musty and bad, denotes the loss of friends, and that some near relation will shortly die.

BRIARS AND BRAMBLES: To dream of these things, foretells you will shortly be in love, and that you will be successful in your pursuits. If you dream you are passing through places covered with these things, it portends troubles; if you are in love, many obstacles will be thrown in the way of your marriage with the present object of your affections; if you are in trade, many difficulties will occur; if you go to sea, storms and shipwreck will overtake you; if they prick you, secret enemies will do you an injury with your friends; and unfavorable tales will make your sweetheart shy of you. If they draw blood of you, expect heavy losses in trade; if you have property at sea it denotes that it will be buried in the waves, if you have lent a sum of money, the person to whom you have lent it will become insolvent and unable to pay you; if you are in love, you will lose your sweetheart; if you dream you pass through them without injury, or any of these consequences, then you will at last triumph over ail your enemies and become happy; you will marry your sweetheart and have many children, who will all do well.

BRIDGE: To dream you are cross over a bridge, is a good omen, it denotes prsperity through life, and success in love. To dream you are passing under a bridge, indicates that you will never be perfectly at ease, that in no undertaking you will have complete success, but that many difficulties wall attend you through life; if you are in love, be careful, for depend you are not the object preferred by your sweetheart, and if you marry, you may be made very unhappy; if you meet with any obstruction on the bridge it foretells a fit of sickness; to the lover it denotes that your sweetheart will be afflicted with illness. To dream a bridge breaks down with you, denotes sudden death.

BROTH: To dream you are eating broth, is a good omen, denotes success in business; it you are soliciting a place, you will purely obtain it; if you are nick, you will speedily recover; if you are in love, you will be successful in your amour; if you are a farmer, you will have a good crop.

NEW DREAM BOOK

BROTHER: To dream you see your brother, denotes a speedy marriage in your family, and that the dreamer will be long lived. If you are in love it is a favorable omen.

BUILDINGS: To dream of being among buildings denotes that you will change your present place of residence, and that you will make many new friends in life; if you are in love, it foretells your sweetheart is about to move at a distance from you, and that you will be in danger of losing the affections of your lover by new faces.

BULLS: To dream you are pursued by a bull, denotes that many injurious reports will be spread of your character, and that you will be in danger of losing your friends; if you are in love, your sweetheart will be in some great danger, and you will narrowly escape some heavy misfortune. If you dream the bull gores you, or tosses you, then expect shortly to lose your liberty; it denotes that some person high in power will do you an injury; if you are in love, never expect to merry the object of your affections; if you are a married man, expect uneasiness in your family.

BUTCHERS: To dream of seeing butchers, is in general a very unlucky omen; it always foretells some injury to the dreamer; if you are in love, it denotes disappointment; if you are in trade, some sharper will defraud you; if you are a farmer, distempers will break out among your cattle; if you are sick, it foretells speedy death; if you see them cutting up meat some of your friends will be hanged, and you will experience much misery and poverty.

BATTLE: To dream you see a battle in the streets forewarns you against secret enemies, who will endeavor to harm you; if you are in love, your sweetheart is false to you.

CAIN: To ddream of this first born son of man, who was Adam's eldest son, is a very unfavorable omen; it denotes much strife from the misconduct of children, and that you will be in danger of losing your liberty; if you are in love it foretells that your sweetheart is deceiving you; that if you marry the present one you will never be happy; and that sour children will be undutiful, and lead you into many troubles and difficulties. After such a dream, I would advise the dreamer to travel into another part of the country, and form new connections.

CAGE: To dream of letting birds out of a cage, denotes a speedy marriage; to a person in business, it denotes success, and to a farmer, it denotes good crops

CAKES: To dream you are eating of cakes, denotes happiness and prosperity; if you are in love, your s wee heart will be kind, faithful, and will marry you; if you are married, it denotes an increase of children.

CANDLES: To dream you see candles burning denotes, if they burn clear and bright, that you will be speedily married; but it also denotes quarreling and trouble; if in your dream the candles go out, much misfortune will attend you and in the quarrel you will be the loser, if you are in love, it denotes the death of your sweetheart. To dream that many candles are brought in, denotes, that by the interference of friends, all your disputes will be amiably adjusted, and that your sweetheart will recover from a fit of sickness.

CARDS: To dream you are playing at cards, is a sure prognostic that you will be in love and speedily married. If you hold a great many picture cards, your marriage will be the means of making you rich and happy. If your cards are mostly diamonds, the person you marry will be of a sour and disagreeable temper; if they are mostly hearts, your marriage will cement love, and you will be very happy and have many children. If they are mostly clubs, you will get money by your marriage; if they are mostly spades, your marriage will turn out very unhappy, and your children will be undutiful and subject to many hardships; if you are in expectation of a place, you will get it; and if you are in business, it will be successful.

CARROTS: To dream of this valuable vegetable denotes prosperity in life; if you have children, they will all thrive; if you are in love, your suit will be successful. If a maiden dreams of carrots, it denotes that she will marry her present sweetheart, have many children, and be very happy. To a farmer it denotes abundant crops.

CATS: To dream of these domestic animals, is indicative of much trouble and vexation; it denotes to the lover, that your sweetheart is treacherous; if you keep servants, they are unfaithful and will rob you. To dream you kill a cat, denotes that you will discover a thief, and prosecute him to conviction; expect also to lose your own liberty through the insincerity of some pretended friend.

CATTLE: To dream you see cattle feeding, denotes great prosperity and unexpected success; to a lover, it foretells a happy marriage, with many children, and to the man it shows that his wife will receive some unexpected legacy. To dream you are driving cattle, denotes that you will become rich by industry; if you are in love, it shows that you have many rivals but that you will distance them all. To dream you see fat cattle, also denotes a plentiful year. To dream you see lean and hungry cattle denotes scarcity and famine.

CHAINS: To dream you see chains denotes that enemies are endeavoring to harm you. But that you will escape their contrivances; if you are in love, it denotes you will marry the present object of your affections; for a maiden to dream of chains, is a certain symptom that she will soon fall in love and be married.

CHICKENS: To dream of a hen and chickens is the forerunner of ill luck, your sweetheart will betray you and marry another; if you area farmer, you will have a bad crop, and lose many of your poultry; if you are in trade some sharper will defraud you; if you go to sea, you will lose your goods and narrowly escape shipwreck.

CHILDREN: To dream you see children denotes success in your undertakings. If you are in trade, you will increase in wealth and industry; if you are in love, our sweetheart will be true to you. To dream you see a child born, denotes a speedy marriage, and that you will be very happy with your family. To dream you see a child die, tells that you will experience some very heavy misfortune, and that your sweetheart will marry another. To dream you see children dirty and ragged, denotes that some friend will endeavor to prevail on you to commit an act, by which your reputation will be endangered; it also denotes that you will be in prison, and experience poverty. For a maiden to dream she is with child, denotes that some man will make an attempt to rob her of her chastity, and that if she resists, she will marry and be very happy.

CHURCH: To dream of a church is portentous of evil. If you are in a church during divine service, you will be engaged in a lawsuit, or some quarrel, that will go very near to ruin you; if you are in love, your sweetheart is unfaithful, and prefers another; if you expect a place, it forebodes disappointment; if you are in trade you will never thrive in your present situation.

CLOCK: To dream you hear the clock strike, denotes that you will be speedily married, and that you will be moderately successful in life. To dream you are counting the hours, if in the forenoon, shows much happiness, and that your sweetheart is true to you, but if in the afternoon. That misfortune and danger will attend you and that your sweetheart is false and loves another.

COACH: To dream you are riding in a coach is a very unlucky omen; it foretells poverty and disgrace; if you are in love, your sweetheart will be idle and bad tempered; if you are in trade, you will become bankrupt; and if you are a farmer your goods will be seized for rent; it also denotes that the dreamer will shortly be in a prison.

CLIMBING: To dream you are climbing up a tree, denotes that you will arrive at some honor in the state, and that you will be successful in life; if you are in love, you will marry your sweetheart after a long courtship. To dream you are climbing up a very steep hill or place foretells many difficulties in life, and much sickness; if you reach the top, you will overcome all your difficulties, or recover from some illness; but if you awake before you have attained the top, you will be disappointed in love and all other projects in life and die in your next illness.

COALS: To dream of coals is a very unlucky omen. If you are in love, your sweetheart will prove false; and endeavor by every means to do you an injury; if you are in trade, it forebodes loss of business; to the farmer it denotes scarcity and want; to the sailor, loss and shipwreck. To dream you see coals burning, if they are very clear and bright, is a good sign, it informs the lover, that your sweetheart is kind and true, that you will marry, have children, and be very happy. If you are soliciting a place, expect speedily to get it; to the trader and farmer it denotes prosperity and success. To dream you see the coals extinguished and reduced to cinders, denotes death, either to yourself or some near relation or friend; it also indicates great losses, and forewarns you of beggary and a prison.

COAL PIT: To dream you are in a coal pit, foretells that you will shortly lead a widow to the hymeneal altar; to a maid it denotes a speedy marriage with her sweetheart, who will become rich and rise to honors in the state; to the trader, it indicates that he will shortly be tricked out of a quantity of goods.

COMETS: To dream you see one of these extraordinary ethereal substances, is ominous of war, plague, famine and death; to the lover it forebodes an entire frustration of his hopes; to the farmer, failure of crops, and to the seaman, storms and shipwreck; after such a dream, change, if possible your present place of residence.

CORN: To dream you see fields of corn, or that you are among unthrashedcorn, in a very favorable omen, it denotes success in business; to the lover, it announces that your sweetheart is kind, of an amiable disposition, that you will marry, have many children, and become rich and happy; if you are a sailor it denotes a lucrative voyage and fine weather, and that you will be near marrying in the next port you touch at. If you are soliciting a place, you may be sure of obtaining it, and rising to honors and preferment. If you dream you are gathering ripe corn, it is the most fortunate dream you can have.

CRANES: To dream you see flock of these birds, is very ominous, it foretells misfortunes and disputes; expect thieves to attack your house, your servants to rob you, your friends to turn against you, and your enemies to gain advantage over you; if you are in love, your sweetheart will betray you; in short, such a dream is the forerunner of evil and I would advise the dreamer to change his quarters as soon as possible, for depend no good will attend him in his present situation.

CROCODILE: To dream you see a crocodile, it is the sure prognostic of misfortune; expect someone will attempt to murder you, that thieves will attack your dwelling, that your sweetheart will prove false, that your business will decay; that your grounds will yield bad crops, that your cattle will be stolen or pounded, that lawsuits will harass and vex you, that storms will overtake you, and pirates rapture your vessels, therefore after such a dream conduct yourself cautiously for it will require all your skill to prevent being totally ruined, and ending your days in a prison.

CROWNS: To dream you see these emblems of royalty portends success and elevation to dignities of either the church or state; for a woman to dream of a crown, shows she will marry a very industrious man, or one who is rich her husband will be prosperous in life, and have many children by her, all of whom will do well except the youngest; if you are in trade you will thrive exceedingly, marry an industrious woman, and become rich. To dream of crown pieces of money, forebodes misfortunes; disappointment in love; prisons, and bad success in trade.

CRUTCHES: To dream you are walking on crutches, is a very unfavorable omen; if you are in love your sweetheart is deceiving; you, and if you marry will make you unhappy; such a dream foretells you will be in prison; that sickness and poverty will attend you, and that in all your undertakings you will fail. To dream you see another walking on crutches, denotes that these things will happen to some friend. If you are a married man, then that your wife is inconstant; if a married woman, then that the husband is ruining himself with some harlot.

CUCUMBERS: To dream of cucumbers, denotes recovery to the sick, that you will fall speedily in love, or that if you are in love, you will marry the present object of your affection. It also denotes moderate success in trade to the sailor they foretell a pleasant voyage, and a sweetheart in a distant climate.

DAIRY: To dream you are in a dairy busy at work, is aver favorable omen. To the maid, it indicates that her lover will be of an industrious turn, and that if she marries, she will have children, and be very happy, and that her husband will become rich, and rise to honors. To the sailor, it denotes that in his next voyage he wilt meet with some unexpected success, and if he is unmarried, that he will get a wife in a far distant country. To the farmer it denotes that some accident will happen through the medium of one of his teams, that his crops will be abundant, but that he will lose some of his live stock either by distemper or thieves. If you are in expectancy of preferment of any kind, it is a very favorable dream, and also denotes success in marriage, trade, and every other undertaking. To a woman with child, it denotes a boy.

DANCING: To dream you are dancing at a ball, wake or entertainment, foretells that you will shortly receive some joyful news from a long absent friend, and that you are about to inherit some unexpected legacy. It foretells success and happiness in love, that your sweetheart is kind and true, and will make you very happy in marriage. To the sailor, it demotes a pleasant and successful voyage, increase of children to married persons, and of business to those in trade.

DARKNESS: To dream you are in a very dark place, or that you are in the dark, is a very unfavorable omen. To the lover it denotes the loss of our sweetheart. To the trader loss of debts, business, and a prison. To the farmer bad crops, to the sailor, shipwreck and misfortune; To dream you get out of darkness into light, denotes good to the dreamer- if you are in prison, you will speedily be released. If you are accused of a crime, you will be acquitted with honor. If you are in poverty, it foretells you will rise to riches and honor. If you are in love, it denotes a happy marriage, and many children, with an industrious husband or wife, expect also to hear some glad tidings from a far distant country.

DEATH: To dream you see this grim looking bundle of bones denotes happiness and long life, that you will either be speedily married yourself, or else assist at a wedding. To dream that you are dead also denotes a speedy marriage and that you will be successful in all your undertakings. To those who are married it foretells young children, and that they will be dutiful, and give you great comfort. To dream you see another person dead, denotes ill usage from friends. If you are in love, your sweetheart will prove false, if you are in trade, sharpers will take you in. If you are a farmer, you will lose money by horses, and be waylaid as you return from market.

DEER: To dream you see deer in a park denotes war and famine. To the lover it foretells some very unpleasant dispute with your sweetheart. To the tradesman, it denotes trouble, and a prison through a quarrel with your creditors. To the seaman, it denotes bad success, and a stormy voyage; expect after such a dream to quarrel with your friends, and be much injured by it.

DEVIL: To dream of this professed enemy to the human race, denotes that many dangers will threaten you all of which you will overcome. It foretells a lawsuit, in which your adversary will endeavor to secretly undermine you, nevertheless you will get he better of him, and put him to shame; if you are in love, it forebodes that some one is endeavoring to alienate the affections of your sweetheart but will be unsuccessful; to the tradesman it denotes a great deal of business attended with many troubles, and the poor it denotes good employment, and to the sailor, a wife with a great sum of money.

DICE: To dream you are playing at dice or backgammon, denotes much good to the dreamer. Expect to marry the present object of your affections, to be very happy, and to become rich; it foretells a good legacy; to the farmer it denotes a very good crop, especially of hay. If you are in trade you will succeed and arrive at riches and honor.

DIRT: To dream of being in the dirt or mire, or that you are in a bog, or that you are traveling near a very dirty road, or that your clothes and flesh are very dirty, is a very unfavorable omen- it portends sickness and misfortune; if you have a good place, expect to lose it; if you are in love expect your sweetheart to discard you; if you are in trade, expect heavy losses, and to be quite reduced; if you are going to sea, it certainly forewarns you of shipwreck and a loss of goods; it also denotes, that the rent of your house or land will be raised upon you.

DITCHES: To dream of deep ditches, steep mountains, rocks and other eminences, surely foretells danger and misfortune; expect thieves to rob your dwelling; that your children will be undutiful, and bring you into trouble; if you are in love it foretells unhappiness if you marry your present sweetheart; if you are in trade, it denotes loss of goods, if not of liberty.

DOGS: To dream of these domestic and faithful animals, has very different significations, according to the manner in which you see them. If they fawn and fondle upon you, then it is a lucky omen; if you have had any quarrel with a friend or sweetheart, it will be reconciled to your advantage; if you are in love, your sweetheart will marry you and render you very happy; it denotes health, riches, and honor. If they are barking and snarling at you, then depend that enemies are secretly endeavoring to destroy your reputation and happiness; if you are in love, be careful of your present sweetheart, if you marry him or her you will be unhappy and poor. If you dream they bite you, then it is a certain prognostic that you will experience some loss, if you are in love, your sweetheart will deceive you, and make you very unhappy.

DOLPHINS: To dream you see dolphins playing in the water, denotes the loss of your sweetheart, and the death of some near relation or friend; it is an unfavorable dream, and signifies that your present pursuits will not be for your advantage, the dreamer would do well to quit his present habitation.

DROWNING: To dream you are drowning, or that you see another drowned or drowning, portends good to the dreamer, and denotes that he will escape many difficulties, settle near his native place, marry, have children, and become happy and rich, to the lover, it denotes that your sweetheart is good tempered, and inclined to marry you; if you area sailor, it foretells a favorable and pleasant voyage.

DRUNKENESS: To dream you are drunk, is one of those dreams by which the dreamer is forewarned of that of which at present he knows nothing- it denotes, that some person whom yet you do not know will become a very good friend, and promote your welfare, that through his means you will acquire riches and honors. To a woman, it denotes that she will be beloved by a man, whom yet she has not seen, who will, if she marries him, make her very happy; and to a man, it denotes that he is tenderly beloved by a woman whom he does not at present think of, who will make them extremely happy, and bring him money,

EAGLES: To dream you see an eagle soaring very high in the air, denotes prosperity, riches, and honor; to the lover, it foretells success in love, and an happy marriage. To dream you see an eagle perched on the steeple of a church, or op any other high eminence, is a very good omen, it denotes that in some arduous undertaking you will be successful, and thereby arrive at riches and honor; it also denotes that the dreamer will make his fortune beyond the sea. If a woman with child dreams of an eagle, then it denotes that the offspring then in her womb will arrive at some very dignified situation, will marry well and be very happy.

EARTHQUAKE: To dream of an earthquake, warns you that your affairs are about to take a very great change. If you see many houses tumbled into ruins, then it will be much for the better; should the houses appear to stand, then for the worse, it always denotes changes in the government, in which the dreamer is much interested; for the lover, it foretells that your sweetheart is about to take a journey, and that it is a great chance if you ever see each other again.

EATING: To dream you are eating, is a very unfavorable omen, it portends disunion among your family, losses in trade, and disappointment in love, storms and shipwreck by sea. To dream you see others eating, is of a contrary tendency and foretells success in all your present enterprises, that your sweetheart is kind and faithful, and that if you marry the present object of your affections, that you will grow rich, be happy, and have dutiful children.

ECLIPSE OF THE SUN: To dream you see an eclipse of the sun, denotes that you will lose some male friend, your father if he be alive; and that you will experience some uneasiness by the means of some treacherous friend; to a woman with child, it foretells a son, who will be a great man.

ECLIPSE OF THE MOON: To dream you see an eclipse of the moon, denotes that you will lose some female friend, your mother if she be living; you will experience great uneasiness on account of a woman; your sweethaart will be unfaithful; poverty will overtake you, and misery end your days. If a woman with child dreams of it, it denotes the fruit of her womb to be a girl, who will be betrayed in love, but who will afterwards marry, have children, and be very happy.

EGGS: To dream you are buying of eggs, is a very favorable omen; whatever you are then about will succeed, whether it be love, trade, or getting a place. To dream you are selling eggs, is also unlucky; if you sell them for gold, your sweetheart will marry you and your children will become wealthy, and be a great comfort to your old age; if you sell them for silver you will be happy in marriage, have many children mostly girls, who will marry well and be happy- it also denotes success in trade and prosperity to the farmer.

To dream that you are eating of eggs, denotes that you will shortly beget a child, and that your affairs will go well. To dream your eggs are broken, denotes loss of goods, quarrels, and poverty; if you are in love it forebodes a separation betwixt you and your sweetheart.

ELEPHANTS: To dream of an elephant, is a very fortunate dream, it denotes luck in the lottery, an acquirement of riches; if you are in love, it denotes a speedy marriage with your sweetheart, and many children, chiefly boys, who will distinguish themselves by their learning,

EVE: To dream you see this mother of all men, who tempted Adam with an apple, and occasioned the fall of man, is a favorable omen; it denotes great happiness to the lover with your present sweetheart; if you are in trade it shows that you will be successful, if you are a farmer, it denotes good crops, and a great increase of your livestock; to a woman with child, it foretells a good labor, and that the child in her womb is boy, who will become a great man. Should she speak to you, be sure you pay great attention to what she says, as it will materially affect your happiness to follow her advice.

EYES: To dream you lose your eyes, is a very unfavorable omen; it denotes decay of circumstances, loss of friends, death of relations, and miscarriage in love; if a woman with child dreams of it, it denotes that the child in her womb will be very unhappy, and lose its liberty.

FACE: To dream that your face is swelled, shows that you will accumulate wealth; if you are in love, it denotes that your sweetheart will receive a very unexpected legacy and marry you. To dream you are washing your face, signifies that you will settle some quarrel much to your advantage; if you are in love, it denotes that your sweetheart is of a good temper and loves you; if you are in trade, it foretells much success.

FALL: To dream you fall from any very high place, or from a tree, denotes loss of place and goods, if you are in love, it surely indicates that you will never marry the present object of your affections. To the tradesman, it denotes decline of business; and to the sailor, storms and shipwreck.

FAIR: To dream you are at a fair, is a bad omen, it denotes that some pretended friend is about to do you an injury; if you are in trade keep a keen look out, for some swindler will certainly attempt to defraud you; if you are a farmer, be careful next time you go to market, for some one will waylay you, and attempt to rob you; if you are in love, it denotes that some rival is attempting tr rob you of those, upon whom you have placed your affections.

FEASTING: To dream you are at a feast, denotes that you will meet with many disappointments, particularly in the thing which you are most anxious about; in love, it forebodes much uneasiness between sweethearts, and to them that are married, it foretells undutiful children, with many heavy losses.

FIELDS: To dream you are in green fields, is a very favorable omen- in love it denotes success and happiness; to the tradesman, success and riches; to the sailor, a pleasant and profitable voyage, to the farmer, plenty and health; if you are soliciting any place or favor be sure you will obtain it. To dream you are in plowed fields, forebodes some severe disputes that will be brouoght upon you by some person who has no children; to the lover, it denotes disappointment, to the married, unhappiness and undutiful children; to the tradesman, loss of business and a prison. To dream you are in a meadow covered with flowers is a very favorable omen; to a man it indicates a very handsome wife, who will bring him lovely children, and make him very happy; to a woman, it denotes that she will marry an handsome young fellow, by whom she will have beautiful children, that she will become rich, and live to a good old age; to the tradesman, it betokens success, good orders and riches; if you are soliciting a place or favor, it portends you will surely obtain it.

FIGHTING: To dream you are fighting, denotes to the lover, that you will lose the object of your affections through a foolish quarrel, it also forebodes much opposition to your wishes with loss of character and property. After such a dream, I would advise the dreamer to quit his present situation, because such a dream indicates that you will not prosper in it; to the sailor it denotes storms and shipwreck, with disappointment in love.

FINGERS: To dream you cut your fingers, if they bleed is a very good omen; you will he successful in love, and your sweetheart will prove kind and true; you will get money from a quarter that you least expect, and be successful in your enterprises. If you dream they do not bleed then it denotes damage by a variety of accidents, that lawsuits will attend you and that you will be unsuccessful in most of your pursuits; in love you will not succeed with your present sweetheart, who prefers another. To dream you lose your fingers denotes the loss of friends, servants, goods, trade and sweethearts.

FIRE: To dream of this subtle element, denoted health and happiness to the lover, marriage with the object of your affections, and many children; it also denotes that you will be very angry with some one on a trifling occasion. To dream you see burning lights descending, as it were from heaven, is a very bad sign indeed, it portends some dreadful accident to the dreamer, such as being hanged, losing your head, having your brains dashed out, breaking your legs, getting into prison, or other strange accidents, to the lover, it also denotes the loss of the affections of your sweetheart, the tradesman, bad success in business. To dream that you are burnt by fire, denotes great danger, and that enemies will injure yon; to the sailor, storms and shipwreck.

FISHING: To dream you are fishing, is a sure sign of sorrow and trouble; if you catch any fish you will be successful in love and business; if you catch none, you will never marry your present sweetheart, nor succeed in your present undertakings; if they slip out of your hands after you have caught them, the person you marry will be of a roving disposition, and some pretended friend will deceive you.

FISTULA: To dream you have a fistula, is indicative of much good, it denotes to the lover, that your sweetheart is kind and true, and that if you marry you will be very happy; it denotes to the tradesman a good establishment in business, and lo the sailor, a pleasant and profitable voyage.

FLEAS: To dream you are tormented with these little insects, is of an unfavorable kind; evil and malicious enemies will do you much injury; your sweetheart will prove false, your trade will decay, and poverty overtake you.

FLIES: To dream of a swarm of flies, denotes that you will have many enemies, and be much harassed by your circumstances, it also denotes that your sweetheart is not sincere, and cares but little about you. To dream you kill them, is a very good omen, it denotes success in love and in trade, and that you will overcome many bitter enemies.

FLOODS: To dream of a flood, shews that you will meet with great opposition from rich neighbors, and that a rich rival will attempt to alienate the affections of your mistress; to the tradesman it denotes lawsuits, loss of business, and a prison; to the sailor, it denotes much success by sea, but danger on shore; to the farmer it indicates loss of cattle, and a dispute with his landlord. To dream you are drowned in a flood. denotes that you will quit your native land, and after many hardships and perils return to it rich and happy, that you will marry a pretty woman and have fine children.

FLYING: To dream you are flying, is a very excellent omen- it foretells elevation of fortune, that you will arrive at dignity in the state, and be happy. If you are in love, your sweetheart will be true to you, and if you marry, you will have many children, who will all do well and be very happy. It indicates that you will take a long journey, which will turn out advantageous to you.

FLOWERS: To dream you are gathering flowers, is a very favorable omen; expect to thrive in everything you undertake, and that you will be successful in love, marry happily and have beautiful children; should they wither under your hands

NEW DREAM BOOK

then expect heavy losses in trade; that your sweetheart will die; or if you are married that you will lose your husband or wife, and also your favorite child.

FORTUNES: To dream you make a sudden fortune, is a very bad omen; to the tradesman, it forebodes losses in trade, quarreling with his creditors, and the loss of liberty; to the lover it denotes that your sweetheart does not return your love; to the sailor, it indicates storms and shipwrecks. If you are soliciting a place, you will not be successful. To dream you are adopting the means of acquiring a fortune, is favorable, it portends a good legacy and success in love.

FOUNTAIN: To dream you are at a fountain, is a very favorable omen; if the waters are clear, it denotes riches and honors, and in love, it foretells great happiness in the marriage state, and that your sweetheart is of an amiable disposition, and true to you; but if the waters appear muddy, then it denotes vexation and trouble; disappointment in business, inconstancy in your sweetheart, and misery in the marriage state.

FOX: To dream of this crafty animal, is the forerunner of much difficulty. If you are in love, your sweetheart will turn out of a sour, disagreeable, ill-natured disposition; your children will be undutiful, and involve you in many difficulties; if you are in trade, sharpers will endeavor to defraud you, and over reach you in bargains; if you are a farmer, the next time you go to market you will be in danger of having your pocket picked; if you are a sailor, you will be in danger of being stranded in some distant country.

FOOLISH: To dream you are a fool is a very favorable omen, and imports m u:h good to the dreamer; expect to be successful in all your present undertakings, whether it be in trade, love, or otherwise, if a maiden dreams she is foolish, it is a certain sign that she will soon be married to the youth of her affections and have children, and be very happy. If a married woman dreams she is foolish, it denotes that she will shortly have a son, who will rise to dignity in the state, be a great friend to the poor, and become very rich.

FRIEND: To dream you see a friend dead, betokens hasty news of a joyous nature; if you are in love, it foretells a hasty marriage with the object of your affections.

FROGS: To dream of frogs, is a very favorable omen; to the farmer, it foretells good crops, and an increase of his livestock; to the tradesman, it denotes success in business; to the lover, a faithful sweetheart; to the married an increase of children, who will be very happy; to the sailor pleasant and prosperous voyages, with a wife in a distant country.

FRUIT: To dream of fruit has a different interpretation according to what the fruit is that you dream of. For the sake of enabling our readers more readily to discover the meaning of their dreams, we have arranged the different fruits alphabetically with their explanations.

Almond: Difficulties, loss of liberty and deceit in love; bad weather to the sailor, and want of success to the tradesman.

Apricots: Denotes health and prosperity, a speedy marriage, dutiful children, and success in love.

Apples: Betokens long life and success, a boy to a woman with child, faithfulness in your sweetheart, and riches by trade.

Cherries: Indicate disappointment in life, vexation in the marriage state, and slight in love.

Currants: Prefigure happiness in life, success in undertakings, constancy in your sweetheart, handsome children to the married, and riches to the farmer and tradesman.

Elderberries: Augur content and riches; to a maiden, they bespeak a speedy marriage, to a married woman, that she will shortly be with child; to the tradesman, success in business; to the farmer good crops.

Figs: Are the forerunner of prosperity and happiness; to the lover; they denote the accomplishement of your wishes, to the tradesman, increase of trade; they are also indicative of a legacy.

Filberts: Forebode much trouble and anger from friends; to the tradesman they denote a prison, and decay of trade; to the lover, a complete disappointment; to the married, care and undutiful children.

Gooseberries: Indicate many children, chiefly sons, and an accomplishment of your present pursuits; to the sailor they declare dangers in his next voyage; to the maiden, a loving husband; and to the man a rakish wife.

Grapes: Betoken to the maiden, that her husband will be a cheerful companion, and a great songster; they denote much happiness a marriage, and success in trade; if you are in love, they augur a speedy union between you and your sweetheart.

Lemons: Denote contentions in your family and uneasiness on account of children; they announce the death of some relation, disappointment in love.

Medlers: Are a very good omen, they bespeak riches to the dreamer; that you will overcome your enemies, and if you have a lawsuit, you will surely gain it- to the lover, they foretell a good husband or wife, with beautiful children, and much happiness.

Melons: Announce speedy recovery to those who are sick; they are indicative of harmony, and inform you, that you will speedily accommodate a dispute between you and others in love. They announce constancy, and in marriage a partner of an happy temper, with handsome children.

Mulberries: Are of good import, to the maiden they foretell a speedy and happy marriage; to the lover, constancy and affection in Ins mistress they also denote wealth, honors, and many children; they are particularly favorable to sailors and farmers.

Nuts: If you see clusters of them, denote riches and happiness; to the lover, success and a good tempered sweetheart; if you are gathering of them, it is not a good omen, for you will pursue some matter that will not turn out to your advantage; if you crack them, the person who courts you, or to whom you pay your addresses, will treat you with indifference, and be very unfaithful.

Nectarines: Are ominous of strife between friends; of riches to the farmer and tradesman, of infidelity in lovers; of children to the married; of bad weather to the sailor; and to the poor they announce plenty and an increase of wages.

Olives: Denote happiness, and that you will be successful in all your present undertakings; to the lover they foretell a speedy marriage with the object of your affections. If you are gathering them off the trees, they then announce much trouble and vexation through friends and children; to the lover, they shew your sweetheart is unfaithful.

Oranges: Are very bad omens; they forebode loss of goods and reputation, attacks from thieves, wounds, and sickness in the object of your affections.

Peaches: Are very favorable to the dreamer; if you are in love, they foretell that your love is returned, that you will marry, have many fine children, and be very happy. They denote riches to the tradesman, and success by sea; also indicates speedy news from a far distant country.

Pears: Prefigure elevation in life, accumulation of riches and honors; success in undertakings, and constancy in lore. If a woman with child dreams of them, she will have a girl, who will marry one far above her rank before she is seventeen; to the maiden, they denote that she will shortly marry a man who will carry her into a distant country, where he will make a great fortune, and return with her to his native land.

Plums: Augur but little good to the dreamer, they are the forerunners of ill luck, and show loss of goods and reputation, they are indicative of infidelity in lovers, and much vexation in the married state.

Pomegranates: Foretell some very unexpected legacy, by which you will be enabled to make a fortune; they denote that your sweetheart is of a good temper, sings well, and is very faithful; to the married, they shew an increase of riches and children, and great success in trade.

Quinces: Are favorable to the dreamer; if you are in a prison, you will be shortly liberated; if you are in trouble, a change will take place that will relieve you from it; if you are sick, you will recover soon; if you are in love, you will marry, and become rich and happy.

NEW DREAM BOOK

Raspberries: Forewarn you of success in your undertakings; of happiness in marriage, of fidelity in your sweetheart, and some news from beyond the sea to your advantage.

Strawberries: Mean to a woman with child, a good time, and a boy; to a maiden, speedy marriage with a man who will become rich, and make her happy; to a youth they denote that his wife will be sweet tempered, and bring him many children, all boys; they foretell riches to the tradesman, and to the sailor; they are a very fortunate dream to the farmer.

Tamarinds: Show much vexation and uneasiness through a woman; bad success in trade; a rainy season, and news from beyond sea that is disagreeable. In love they denote disappointment.

Walnuts.: Portend difficulties and misfortunes in life; if you have children, your eldest son will marry a woman who will make him very unhappy; in love, they foretell infidelity and disappointment; to the seaman storms and shipwreck; to the tradesman, loss of goods and reputation through a confidential servant.

Observe, if you dream of any of these fruits when out of season, or that you are gathering them when green, it denotes sickness- if you dream they are rotten, it foretells poverty. To dream of gathering ripe fruit, when there is plenty, betokens happiness and riches, and the speedy receipt of money. If you gather fruit from an old withered tree, it is a sign that you will unexpectedly inherit the effects of some aged person. To dream you have made yourself sick with eating of fruit, denotes to a woman with child a troublesome and difficult labor, to the tradesman, loss of goods by sharpers, and that without great care you will get into prison; to the lover, it shows that your sweetheart will be of a jealous disposition, and that if you marry, you will be made very miserable through undutiful children.

FUNERAL: To dream of a burying, denotes speedy marriage, and that you will hear of the death or imprisonment of some near relation or esteemed friend; they also foretell the acquisition of wealth, and that an estate will fall to you from a distant relation by your mother's side. If you see any particular person attending the funeral, either that person, or some friend of his, will die, and leave you something : if there is an hearse with feathers on it, you will marry some rich person yourself, or assist at some relation's wedding, who will marry well, and be a friend to you.

GALLOWS: To dream of the gallows, is a most fortunate omen; it shows that the dreamer will become rich and arrive at great honors; to the lover it shows the consummation of his most sanguine wishes, and that by marriage you will become rich and happy, have many children, particularly a son, who will become a great man, and be the founder of his family's honor; for a woman with child to dream of a gallows, signifies that she is pregnant of a son, will have a good time, and that the then fruit of her womb will become very rich, and have a great employment in the state.

GARDEN: To dream you are walking in a garden, is of a very favorable nature; it portends elevation in fortune and dignity, to the lover it denotes great success, and an advantageous marriage; to the tradesman, it promises increase of business; to the farmer plentiful crops; and to the sailor, pleasant and prosperous voyages.

GEESE: To dream of geese is the forerunner of good. Expect soon to see a long absent friend, they denote success and riches to the dreamer in the furtherance of his pursuits, in love they augur speedy marriage and fidelity in your sweetheart.

GIANTS: To dream of seeing giants, is an omen of good. If you are in trade, you will have great increase of your business from foreign parts, if you are a farmer, your crops will prove abundant, your live stock increase, and an opportunity offer of purchasing the ground you till. If you are in love, your sweetheart is thereby denoted to be of a good temper, faithful and sincere to you, and that if you marry, you will become happy, it also denotes, that you will receive a considerable present from some friend.

GIFTS: To dream you have any thing given you, is a sign that some good is about to happen to you. It also denotes, that a speedy marriage will take place betwixt you and your sweetheart. To dream you have given any thing away, is the forerunner of adversity; and in love, denotes sickness and inconstancy in your sweetheart or partner.

GLASS: To dream of glass, marks inconstancy in your sweetheart, and is ominous of bad success in your undertakings in life. To dream you break glass, shows that your sweetheart will forsake you, and that you will unexpectedly meet with misfortunes and troubles. To dream you receive a glass full of water, is indicative of a speedy marriage, and that you will have many children, who will do well. If the glass appears broken, the death of your sweetheart, or if married, of your spouse is predicted; for a woman with child, or a married man whilst his wife is with child, to dream of breaking a glass of wine or water, denotes that the child in the womb will be preserved after much danger, and perhaps the death of the mother. If either of them dream that they spill the wine or water, it is indicative that the mother will live, but the child die.

GLOBE: To dream you are looking at a globe foretells

much good, and that you will be a great traveler, to the lover it shows that you will not marry your present sweetheart, but that you will take a journey to a distant place, when you will fall in love and will marry, become rich and live happy.

GOLD: To dream of gold is a very good omen, it denotes success in your present undertakings, after experiencing some little difficulties; if you receive gold in bars, you will inherit an estate in a far distant country, and have some trouble in getting possession of it; if you receive guineas or any other gold coin, your affairs will prosper; your sweetheart will be true and marry you, you will have many children and be very happy; if you pay gold, it betokens an increase of friends and business; if you let gold fall, it denotes an attack from thieves; if you are in trade, some swindler will attempt to defraud you; if you pick up gold, it denotes that some quarrel will be settled to your advantage; if you are in prison, it shows you will speedily be enlarged; it also denotes the death of a husband or wife, if you are married, if single, of your sweetheart.

GRAVE: To dream you see a grave, foretells sickness and disappointment; if you are in love, depend you will never marry your present sweetheart; if you go into the grave, it shows you will experience a loss of property, and that fake friends will defame you: if you come out of the grave, denotes success in your undertakings, that you will rise in the world, become rich, and if you are in love, that you. Will speedily marry your sweetheart; if you take another out of the grave, you will be the means of saving the life of a person, who will be a very great friend to you, and receive some unexpected legacy.

GUNS: To dream you see people firing off guns or cannon, augurs that the dreamer will experience much adversity, be shut up in a prison, and be very unsuccessful in your undertakings, in love it shews that your sweetheart will become your enemy. To dream that they are firing at you, shows that you will be exposed to many perilous dangers, such as shipwreck, assassination, or loss of liberty; if you are firing them yourself it foretells that you will be involved in a lawsuit, that will prove very prejudicial to you.

HAIL: To dream you are in a hail storm, presages great sorrows in life, through the divulging of some important secrets : if you are in love, it forewarns you against marrying your present sweetheart, who will prove of a very bad temper, be much inclined to scolding, and make you miserable.

HAIR: To dream you are combing your hair, is a very good omen; it portends success in love, business or any other pursuit, also riches. To dream your hair has grown long, and hangs loose over your shoulders, denotes that you will be beloved by one in a superior condition of life to yourself. To dream it is cut short or that it has fallen off, shows that you will lose a relation or friend by death. To dream you burn your hair, shows that your sweetheart is unfaithful and deceives you.

HANGED: To dream of seeing people hanged, or that you are going to be hanged yourself, denotes that you rise above your present condition by marriage.

HEN AND CHICKS: To dream of a hen and chickens is a very unfavorable omen; it portends loss of property, of friends and reputation. In love it denotes misery and disappointment. After such a dream, I would advise the dreamer to change his residence. To dream you hear a hen cackling, foretells success in love and an accumulation of riches by means of female relations.

HILLS: To dream you are traveling over steep hills, shows that you will encounter many difficulties, and enter upon some arduous undertaking. If you descend the hill easily, you will get the better of all your difficulties and enemies, and become rich; to the lover, it shows rivals, who will give great uneasiness.

HORSES: To dream of these useful animals is symptomatic of good; if you are mounted on a fine pony horse, you will marry a rich person, who will do well and make you happy; it also shows that you will change your situation in life. If you fail from your horse, difficulties will occur, and some unexpected disaster befall you.

HOUSE: To dream of building a house, is a very favorable omen; if you are in trade, it denotes success; if in love, that your sweetheart is good tempered and faithful, and will make you very happy. To dream your house is burnt down denotes much trouble and many difficulties, with loss of goods and reputation. To dream you see your house on fire, foretells hasty news, and that you will lose a near relation.

HUNGER: To dream you are very hungry, is a very favorable omen; it shows that by your genius and industry, you will rise in the world to wealth and honors; it denotes to the lover that your sweetheart will undertake a journey before you marry.

HUNTING: To dream you are hunting a fox, and that he is killed, shows much trouble through the pretensions of false friends, but that you will discover them, and overcome all their machinations; if you are hunting a hare, it is indicative of bad success; you will he disappointed in your favorite object be it what it may; hunting a stag, if he is caught alive, denotes good to the dreamer, and that he will be successful in all his present undertakings.

HUSBANDRY: To dream of the implements of husbandry, has a variety of interpretations. To dream of a plow, denotes success in life and a good marriage. To dream of a yoke is unfavorable unless it be broken, then it denotes a rising above your present condition. To dream of a scythe, shows injury from enemies, and disappointment in love. To dream of a team, denotes death in the family of the dreamer; a sweetheart of a very bad temper, and want of success in undertakings.

ICE: To dream of ice, is a very favorable omen; to the lover, it shows your sweetheart is of an amiable temper, and faithful. To the tradesman, it denotes success and riches; to the farmer, a plentiful harvest. To dream you are sliding or skating on the ice, denotes that you will pursue some unprofitable concern, and be much worsted by your engagements; in love, it shows that your sweetheart is fickle and deceiving, and that you will never marry your present one.

INN: To dream of being in an inn, is a very unfavorable dream; it denotes poverty and want of success in undertakings; expect soon to be yourself, or some of your family committed to prison; if you are sick, it denotes you will never recover; to the tradesman it shews loss of trade and bad servants.

KEYS: To dream of keys, is favorable to a person in trade, and to a sailor; they denote some gift, and that the dreamer will become rich. To dream you lose a key, fore-shows anger, and that you will lose a friend. To dream of finding a key, denotes an addition to your estate. If you are married, it also foretells the birth of a child, if you give another a key, you will be speedily married; in love, keys betoken faithfulness, and a good tempered sweetheart.

KISSING: To dream you are kissing a pretty maid is indicative of good, it denotes that some unexpected friend will do you a great kindness; in love it shews that your sweetheart places her affections on you and you alone, and that if you marry you will be happy; in the tradesman, it denotes riches and augmentation of business through the means of women. For a woman to dream she is kissed by a man and that she is enjoyed after resistance, shows she will be speedily married to the man who courts her and that she will be very happy, if the enjoyment is complete. If not, and she is interrupted, it shows that her husband will be cross and ill humored. To dream of kissing a married woman, and that she consents to it, is indicative of much sorrow and poverty, and that you will fail of success in all your present undertakings.

KNIVES: To dream of knives, is a very unpropitious omen; it betokens lawsuits, poverty, disgrace, strife, and a general failure in the pursuit of your projects. In love, it shows that your sweetheart is of a bad temper, and unfaithful, and that if you marry, you will live in enmity and misery.

LABOR: To dream you are hard at work, shows that you will go on a long, dangerous, and unprofitable journey; if you sweat, it denotes that you will fall sick on the road. To dream that a woman is in labor and that she is delivered of a dead child, is a very unfavorable omen; it denotes that you will undertake some business which you will never bring to a happy conclusion, but by which you will be a considerable loser. If she has a good time, and is delivered of a living child, then it is favorable; you will be successful in your undertaking; acquire riches, marry the person you love, have children and be very happy.

LADDER: To dream you climb a ladder, is a very good prognostic; it denotes that you will better your situation in life, and arrive at honors in the state; in love, it denotes a happy marriage with the object of your affections, and that you will become by industry rich, and settle your children happily.

LEAPING: To dream you are leaping over walls, bars or

gates, is a sign that you will encounter many difficulties in your present pursuits, and that your sweetheart will not marry you; if you are leaping over ditches, drains, or hedges, it is a favorable omen, you will be successful in love, trade or other concerns; it also denotes that you will enter into partnership with more than one person, by which you will accumulate riches and become very respectable.

LETTER: To dream of receiving letters is demonstrative of your being beloved by a person of the opposite sex, who is very much your friend, and will do all in their power to make you happy. To dream of writing letters, shows success in enterprises, and that you will receive some very pleasant news.

LICE: To dream that you are lousy, and that you are killing a great many of them, is a very good omen; it denotes great riches to the dreamer after many severe misfortunes and much sickness; they also portend deliverance from enemies, and that you will overcome much slander and malice; that in love you will succeed and be very happy, after a long and tedious courtship.

LIGHT: To dream you see a great light, is a happy presage, it denotes that you will attain to great honors, and become very rich; in love, shows a sweetheart of an amiable disposition, that you will marry well, have children, and be very happy; if the light disappears all in a sudden, it betokens a great change in your present situation, much for the worse: it portends imprisonment and great loss of goods, with unexpected misfortunes.

LION: To dream of seeing this king of beasts denotes that you will appear before your betters and that you will be promoted to some lucrative office, accumulate riches, and marry a woman of great spirit; it augurs success in trade, and prosperity from a voyage by sea.

LINEN: To dream you are dressed in clean linen, denotes that you will shortly receive some glad tidings that your sweetheart is faithful and will marry you; that you will be successful in your present undertakings, and that you will receive a handsome present from an agreeable youth. If your linen is checkered, you will get a legacy from some friend, and marry a very industrious person. If it is dirty, then it denotes poverty, a prison, and disappointment in love, with the loss of something valuable.

MAD: To dream you are mad, or that you are in company with mad people, is very good to the dreamer; it promises to us; life, riches, happy marriage, success in trade and good children; if you are a farmer, some accident will happen to part of your livestock, but you will have plentiful crops. If you have a lawsuit, it will be determined greatly in your favor.

MARRIAGE: To dream you are married is ominous of death, and very unfavorable to the dreamer; it denotes poverty, a prion, and misfortunes. To dream you assist at a wedding, is the forerunner of some pleasing news and great success. To dream of lying with your newly married husband or wife, threatens danger and sudden misfortunes, and also that you will lose a part of your property; to the sailor, it denotes storms and shipwreck, with a narrow escape from death.

MEAT: To dream you are buying raw meat, signifies that friends will step forward and be of great assistance to you, that you will overcome difficulties, and acquire riches. To dream you are buying dressed meat, denotes that you will receive a legacy, but have some misfortune by traveling. To dream you only see raw meat, denotes that you will have a great quarrel; for a maid to dream of raw meat, denotes, if she gets it, a speedy marriage, if not, that she will be disappointed.

MILK: To dream you are selling milk, denotes that you will be crossed in love, and that you will be unsuccessful in trade. To dream you are drinking of milk, is the forerunner of joyful news and great success; if you are giving milk away, it shows that you will be successful in love, and marry happily, have many children and do very well. To see milk flowing from the breast of a woman, denotes success in trade; and in love, that you will have many children, and that they will become rich through the industry of their parents.

MICE: To dream of mice denotes prosperity and accumulation of riches; success in love, and happy marriage. For a married woman to dream of mice, is a token that she will be with child shortly, and that the fruit of her womb will become very rich and powerful; to the farmer, they denote plentiful crops, and an increase of live stock.

MIRE: To dream you stick fast in the mire is a very unfavorable omen, it presages a prison, and many difficulties and misfortunes; it shows that you will marry a person who will reduce you to great poverty, and that you will be charged with an heinous offense, and suffer much great calamity.

MONEY: To dream of receiving money is a very good omen, it denotes success in your undertakings; in love it foretells a speedy marriage and many children. If you dream you lose money, it is a proof you w ill be deceived in love, and be unsuccessful in some favorite pursuit. To dream you are paying money foretells the birth of a son, destined to cut a great figure in life; if you have a lawsuit, you will gain it; if you are in love, you will be successful. If in trade, you will become rich; if you are soliciting a place, you will obtain it, and it will lead to one more lucrative.

MONKEYS: To dream of these mischievous creatures is ominous of evil; they announce deceit in love, unfaithfulness in the marriage state, undutiful children, malicious enemies, and an attack by thieves.

MOON: To dream of the moon is a very favorable omen, it denotes sudden and unexpected joy, great success in love, and that the dreamer is tenderly beloved. To dream of seeing the new moon, is good for tradesman, farmers, and lovers; it is the forerunner of success and happiness.

MOTHER: To dream you see your mother, is a certain prognostic of some agreeable adventure being about to happen to you, and that you will hear from a friend at a distance. To dream you see your mother dead forebodes trouble and adversity, and that you will become very poor.

MOUNTAINS: To dream you see steep and craggy mountains, presages difficulties in accomplishing your designs; if you ascend them and gain the top you will be successful in whatever you undertake, become very rich, and arrive at great honors in the state; to a maid, they denote that she will marry a man who will become great and powerful and that her children will be people of consequence.

MUSIC: To dream you hear delicious music is a very favorable omen; it denotes joyful news from a long absent friend; to married people it denotes sweet tempered children; in love, it shows that your sweetheart is very fond of you, is good tempered, sincere and constant. Rough and discordant music foretells trouble, vexation and disappointment.

MYRTLE TREE: To dream you see a very fine myrtle-tree, is a sign you will soon he in love; that you will have many amours, and be successful. It denotes constancy in your sweetheart; to a maid, it bespeaks marriage, and great happiness in that state.

NAILS: To dream your nails are grown very long, is very good, and denotes riches, prosperity and happiness; great success in love; a good industrious husband or wife, with dutiful children. It also foretells that you will suddenly receive a sum of money that will be of great use to you.

NAKEDNESS: To dream you see a naked woman is very lucky, it foretells that some unexpected honors await you; that you will become very rich, and be successful in most of your undertakings. To dream you see a naked man is indicative of trouble and attack by thieves, loss of goods and reputation. For a maid to dream she sees a naked man, shows that she will quickly fall in love and be married, and that. she will have many male children, who will be great cowards.

NIGHTINGALE: To dream of this pretty warbler, is the forerunner of joyful news; great success in business; of plentiful crops, and of a sweet tempered lover. For a married woman to dream of a nightingale, shews that she will have children, who will be great singers.

OLD MAN: For a woman to dream she is courted by an old man, is a sure prognostic that she will receive a sum of money, and be successful in her undertakings. For a maid to dream of it, shows that she will many a rich young fellow, will have many children by him, who will all become rich.

OLD WOMAN: For a man to dream he is courting an old woman, and that she returns his love, is a very fortunate omen, it prefigures success in worldly concerns; that he will marry a beautiful young woman, have lovely children, and be very happy.

NEW DREAM BOOK

OFFICE: To dream you are turned out of your office foreshadows death and loss of property; to a lover it indicates want of affection in your sweetheart, and misery if you marry the present object of your affections. To a sailor it announces bad weather and shipwreck.

ONIONS: To dream of this vegetable, denotes a mixture of good and bad luck; if you are eating them, you will receive some money, or recover some lost or stolen things, or discover some hidden treasure; your sweetheart will be faithful, but of a cross temper; it also denotes attack from thieves, and a failure of crops; it shows that you will be engaged in some disagreeable quarrels, perhaps with your own family; if you are throwing onions away, it is the forerunner of mischief and quarrels; if you are in love, you will fall out with your sweetheart; if you are in trade, you will quarrel with your customers and servants; if you are gathering onions, it betokens the recovery of some sick person of your family; the receipt of some unexpected news of a joyful kind, and a removal from your present situation.

ORCHARD: To dream you are in an orchard, denotes that you will become rich by the inheritance of a good legacy; that you will marry much to your advantage. For a married person to dream of being in an orchard, shows an increase of children, and that they will become rich and live happy; it also denotes that you will have a son, who will rise to great preferment in the state, and be a great friend to the poor; in love, it denotes affection and constancy in your sweetheart, and that you will travel before you marry.

OVEN: To dream you see an oven, foretells that you are about to be separated from your family by changing your present residence; it shows you an attack by thieves in some by place and also that your sweetheart is of a roving and fickle disposition, little likely to make you happy.

OWL: To dream of this bird of night is a very bad omen, it foretells sickness, poverty, imprisonment, and want of success in your undertakings; it also forewarns you that some male friend will turn out perfidious, and endeavor to do you a very great injury, in which without the utmost caution on your part he will succeed.

OYSTERS: To dream you are eating oysters is a very favorable omen; if you are in trade, your business will increase very fast, and you will become rich; if you are a farmer, you will have plentiful crops; if you are married, your wife or husband will be very fond of you, and you will have many line children. For a maid to dream of eating oysters, shows that she will quickly be married to a young man who will thrive much by his industry, and have many children by her; to a man, it denotes that he will marry a real virgin who will be very fond of him, and bring him many children. If you dream that the fish falls off the shell, it denotes disappointment in your expectations, and that you will lose the affections of the person you confide in. It also denotes much trouble to your children, one of whom will lose his liberty.

PALM: To dream you are gathering of palm denotes plenty, riches, and success in undertakings, and is a very good omen indeed; to a married woman it is a certain token of her bearing children; to a maid, it foretells a sudden marriage with the youth she loves; that she will have children by him, and that she will live very happy in the marriage state.

PAPER: To dream of paper is a good omen; if it is quite clean, you will be very successful in your undertakings; marry the person you love, have good and dutiful children, and be very happy; if it is dirty or scribbled upon, then it shows temporary want, and some unpleasant altercations; if it is fairly written, you will receive hasty news of a good nature, make an advantageous bargain, and obtain some money by a legacy; if it appears rumpled and careless folded up, it shows, that some difficulties will occur which will give you much pain; if it is neatly folded, you will obtain your favorite wish, be what it may.

PATHS: To dream you are walking in a broad good pathway, denotes health and success in undertaking; in love, it shows you will meet with a sweetheart, who will make you very happy. If you are married, you will obtain your favorite wish. To dream the pathway is crooked, rugged and uneven, is the forerunner of mischief, poverty, and trouble; it is a sign that your bosom friend will betray you; if you are married, it marks infidelity in your partner, and shews want of success in undertakings, decrease of business, failure of crops, storms, and shipwreck.

PEACOCK: To dream of seeing this beautiful bird is a very good omen, it denotes great success in trade; to a man a very beautiful wife, much riches and a good place; to a maid, a good and rich husband; to a widow, that she will be courted by one who will tell her many fine tales, without being sincere; it also denotes great prosperity by sea, and an handsome wife in a distant part.

PICTURES: To dream you are looking at beautiful pictures, foreshadows that you will be allured by false appearances into some unprofitable concern that you will waste your time on some idle projects and that you will always be in pursuit of happiness without attaining it. In love, it denotes great pleasure in the enjoyment of the beloved object; it promises a handsome wife, a good husband, and beautiful children.

PIGEONS: To dream you see pigeons flying import

hasty news of a very pleasant nature, and great success in undertakings; they are very favorable to lovers, as they announce constancy in your sweetheart, but also that the person you love will be absent from you a long while on a journey; if your lover is at sea, they denote that he has a, pleasant voyage, continues faithful, and will return rich.

PIT: To dream of falling into a deep pit, shows that some very heavy misfortune is about to attend you; that your sweetheart is false and prefers another; to a sailor, it forebodes some sad disaster at the next port you touch at. To dream you are in a pit, and that you climb out of it without much trouble, foreshadows that you will have many enemies, and experience much trouble, but that you will overcome them and surmount your difficulties, marry well, and will become rich; to a sailor, it denotes that he may experience shipwreck, and be cast on a foreign shore, where he will be hospitably received, fall in love, and marry a rich and handsome wife, quit sea, and live at ease, on shore.

PLAYS: To dream you are at a play, is the forerunner of great good luck, it betokens great happiness in the marriage state, and success in business; to a maid, it shows speedy marriage with a young man who will be very successful in life, acquire riches and honors, and make her happy.

PEN: To dream you see a pond with clear water in it, betokens great success in your unuertakings; to a man, it denotes his being beloved by a beautiful woman; to a maid, it shows the constancy and affection of her swain, with great prosperity after marriage; to a married woman, that she will be quickly pregnant; if there appears many fish she will have twins; if the fish are small, her next will be a girl, if large, a boy; to a widow, it denotes that she will marry again and be very happy.

PURSE: To dream of finding a purse is a very favorable omen, it denotes great happiness and unlooked for prosperity; in love, it is the sure token of a speedy marriage, and the being dearly beloved by the object of your affections. To dream you lose your purse, shows the loss of a friend; in other respects it denotes some pleasant adventure is about to happen to you, by which you will be the gainer; to the sailor, it denotes the loss of his sweetheart whilst at sea.

QUARRELING: To dream you are quarreling, denotes that some unexpected news will reach you, and that your sweetheart is about to be married to another; it shows success in business, although you are opposed by many enemies who pass for your friends.

RACING: To dream you are running a race, is a token of good, presages much success in life, and that you will speedily hear some joyful news; in love, it denotes that you will conquer all your rivals, and be happy in the union with the object of your affections. To dream you are riding a race, shows disappointment and anger, bad success in trade and in love; to a married woman it denotes the loss of her husband's affections, and that her children will be in trouble.

RAIN: To dream of being in a shower of rain, if it be gentle and soft, denotes great success in your present undertakings. It is particularly favorable to lovers, as it denotes constancy, affection, and a sweet temper. To the sailor it promises good fortune by sea, and that he will marry a beautiful girl, be happy, and have many children; if it be very heavy rain, accompanied by thunder and lightning, then expect to be assailed by thieves, and to experience disappointments and misfortunes; such a dream denotes inconstancy and perfidy in your lover, and that another is prefered.

NEW DREAM BOOK

RAINBOW: To dream you see a rainbow, denotes great traveling and change of fortune; it also foretells sudden news of a very agreeable nature, it announces that your sweetheart is of a good temper and very constant, and that you will be very happy in marriage, have great success business through the means of trading with foreign parts.

RATS: To dream of seeing rats, is the sign of; having many enemies, and that you are exposed to many dangers from pretended friends. If you are attacked by them, and get the better, it betokens that you will overcome your difficulties, destroy your enemies, and arrive at preferment; if they should tear you and make you run away, then, expect some very heavy misfortune will happen to you; that you will be attacked by thieves, and that enemies will compass your destruction, that you will get into prison and become very poor.

RAVENS: To dream you see a raven is a very unfavorable token, it denotes mischief and adversity; in love, it shows falsehood, and to the married they forebode much mischief through the adultery of your conjugal partner; to the sailor, they betoken shipwreck, and much distress on a foreign shore.

READING: To dream you are reading an agreeable book, indicates that you will be successful in your love, and that you will become very rich in trade, it is very propitious; to the sailor it denotes that in a distant country a rich woman will make his fortune, and be very food of him; if you are in prison, it denotes a speedy emancipation, and a lucrative situation.

RIDING: To dream you are riding, if it be with a woman, is very unfortunate; expect lo be crossed in love; if you are in trade, business will decay, and you will be very near bankruptcy; if you are a sailor, it denotes perfidy in your sweetheart, and loose conduct with one of your shipmates, but if it be with men, then expect the reverse of these things will happen and that you will obtain a sum of money by some speculation of which you have but an indifferent opinion.

RING: To dream of a ring is favorable if it be on your finger; if you are in in love, expect to be speedily united to the person on whom you have placed your affections; if in trade, expect to form a profitable connection with a person you have not yet seen; if you are a sailor, you will meet with some unexpected success in a distant country in your next voyage. To dream your ring falls off your finger, betokens evil and a prison, also the death of some near friend or relation; to a woman with child, it shows that the child of which she is then pregnant will encounter many difficulties and be far from being happy; to the maiden, it is a warning to beware of her present lover, who will try to rob her of her virginity, and if be succeeds abandon her.

RODS: To dream you are whipped with rods, denotes that you will meet with a very pernicious friend, who will go very near to ruin you- it also betokens your being shortly at a merry making, where you must be careful of quarreling, if you do, it will turn out to your disadvantage. In love it denotes your sweetheart to be of a fickle disposition, and little calculated to make you happy.

ROSES: To dream of those fragrant flowers during the season which brings them forth, is a certain token of happiness and success- in love they show your sweetheart to be faithful, and that you will marry and have many children- to the sailor, they indicate a pleasant and prosperous voyage, with some unexpected good fortune at sea. To the tradesman and farmer, increase of business and abundant crops. If a married woman dreams of them, she will be shortly with child of a son, who will become a great man, and render his parents very happy. To a maiden, they show her sweetheart to be industrious, and one calculated to make her very happy m the connubial state.

To dream of these flowers when out of season, indicates distress and disappointment. To the tradesman they forebode bankruptcy, and a prison- to the married, loss of their mates and children; to the sailor, shipwreck and storms; to the farmer, bad crops; to the lover, infidelity in your sweetheart.

RIVER: To dream you see a flowing river, and that the waters are smooth and clear, presages happiness and success in life; to the lover it shows constancy and affection in the object of your love, and that if you marry, you will pass a very contented and happy life, have fine children, mostly girls, who will be very beautiful; to the tradesman and farmer, it shows prosperity and gain; to the sailor, that his sweetheart will be kind and constant, and that his next voyage will be lucrative and pleasant. If the water appears disturbed and muddy or has a yellow tinge, then it denotes that you will go to sea, where you will acquire considerable riches; if you have a lawsuit, such a dream surely foretells that you will gain your cause.

SCABS: To dream you are all over scabs, is the sure forerunner of great success and riches; if you are in servitude, expect soon to become master for yourself; if you are in trade, then expect a great increase of business, and that you will arrive at honors in the state; if you have a lawsuit, be sure it will go in your favor, and that you will be a considerable gainer by it; if you are in love depend your sweetheart will have a good legacy shortly. For a maiden to dream she is covered with scabs, foretells that she will speedily be married to a very rich man; if it be a widow who dreams, she will receive a considerable sum of money through the friends of her deceased husband. A sailor is hereby shown that a rich woman will confer great wealth upon him in a distant country, that he will not marry her, but return to his native land, where he will marry a beautiful girl, of poor parents.

SEA: To dream you are sailing on a smooth sea, is a good omen in love, it foretells the happy possession of the beloved object, with many children, and the acquirement of much riches. To dream you are sailing on a rough tempestuous sea, forebodes many difficulties in life, particularly a disappointment in love; if you are in trade, be careful, for some sharper is about to defraud you out of a quantity of goods, and will, without the utmost circumspection on your part succeed. If you are soliciting a place, some one will injure you with your patron. To dream you are cast away, and thrown on a desert rocky shore, indicates that after many troubles and difficulties you will become rich and happy; to the lover, it foretells many rivals, who will give much vexation, but that you will ultimately obtain the object of your affections, have many children, as many girls as boys, who will all do well except the third born, who will either die very young, or else be imprisoned for many years. To dream you are washing or swimming in the sea, is a certain prognostic of heavy losses in trade, particularly by lending money; to the lover, it denotes the loss of your sweetheart by death, or marrying another.

To dream you are on a voyage at sea, and catching fish, shows the death of some friend or relation in a foreign country; to the lover, it presages that your sweetheart will go mad, be confined for lunacy, and there die; to the farmer, it forebodes bad crops, and loss by unfaithful servants. Expect after such a dream to have your house attacked by thieves, and that some person, in whom you repose confidence will deceive you.

SHAVING: To dream you are being shaved or that your head has been shaved, is a very unfavorable omen; in love, it denotes treachery and disappointment: and in the married state infidelity and discord; to the tradesman, it predicts loss of goods and business; to the sailor, an unpleasant and stormy voyage, and that he will be defrauded on a foreign shore. If you have a lawsuit, it shows you that you are sold by your attorney and will surely lose your cause; to the farmer it prefigures bad crops and diseases among his livestock, also that he will be tricked by sharpers at a fair.

SHEEP: To dream you see a flock of sheep feeding is a very favorable omen- it denotes success to the lover, it indicates your sweetheart to be faithful, of an amiable temper, and inclined to marry you. In the married state it denotes children, who will be very happy, become rich, and be great comfort in the evening of life. To the tradesman, it foretells increase of business and accumulation of wealth, but also forewarns him that he has a servant unworthy of his confidence; to the sailor, nothing can be a greater sign of good luck, his next voyage will be pleasant, and lucrative, and his sweetheart kind and true. To dream you see them dispersing, and running away from you, shows that pretended friends are endeavoring to do you an injury, and that your children will meet with persecution and great troubles; in love, such a dream shows your sweetheart to be fickle, and little calculated to make you happy. To dream you see sheep-shearing, is indicative of loss of property, and the affections of the person you love, also of your liberty. To dream you are shearing them yourself, shows that you will gain an advantage over some person that meant to harm you, and that you will get the better of difficulties, and marry the object of your affections.

SHOES: To dream you have a new pair of shoes denotes much success in life, and triumph over enemies; in love they prognosticate speedy marriage and fidelity. In the married state an increase of children. If a maiden dreams she has a pair of new shoes; it denotes that a man will attempt to be rude with her, but that her honor will be saved by the interposition of a stranger, who will either marry her, or some friend of hers. To dream your shoes are worn out and bad, shows decay in circumstances, and loss of friends; in love, it foretells the infidelity of your lover, who will marry another. After such a dream I advise those who can, to change their place of residence, their present situation being hereby denoted to be very unfavorable to them.

SHOOTING: To dream you are out a shooting is favorable if you kill much game; to the lover it shows a mistress kind and good humored, who will make him an excellent and notable wife. To the tradesman and farmer, success and riches, to the sailor wealth acquired in a distant country, but if you dream you kill little or no game, then it presages bad luck, and disappointment in love. To dream you arc shooting with bow and arrows, is a very favorable dream particularly to lovers and tradesmen.

SILK: To dream you see silk, either in pieces or for sewing, signifies prosperity and success in undertakings; to the lover it denotes a sweetheart of an industrious disposition, good tempered and very faithful; in trade it foretells increase of business by means of women. To dream you are clothed in silk, foretells that you will rise to honors in the state, and become rich, but that you will quarrel with a rich neighbor who will endeavor to do you mischief. For a married woman to dream of being dressed in a silk gown, shews her husband is fond of an harlot, who will go near to ruin him. If a maiden dreams of it, she will speedily see her lover.

SILVER: To dream of this valuable metal, shows that false friends are about you, and will attempt your ruin; in love it denotes falsehood in your sweetheart. To dream you are receiving or picking up silver money, if they are small as sixpences, denotes want and a prison; if they are shillings, they indicate the receipt of a small sum of money, and the acquisition of some new friends, but if they are half crowns or crown pieces, then they denote misery, a prison, and bad success in your undertakings, attacks from thieves, and bankruptcy in trade. If a woman with child dreams of silver, it shows she will have a girl and a good time, but the child will grow poor.

SINGING: To dream you are singing, shows that you will hear shortly some very melancholy news; to the lover it denotes your sweetheart to be bad tempered, and of an unfaithful disposition, to the farmer, loss by a hay rick taking fire; to the sailor storms and shipwreck. To dream you only hear singing and merry making shows that you will have some agreeable news from a person long absent. If you are sick, it denotes a speedy recovery; if you are in prison it foretells you will speedily regain your liberty.

SMALLPOX: To dream that you or your children have the small pox, shows that you will accumulate great riches by dirty and disgraceful means, and that you will hear from a long absent friend, who is in confinement; to the lover, it denotes marriage.

SNAKES: To dream you see snakes or serpents shows that you will be imprisoned and encounter many dangers; if you are in love, your sweetheart will be false. To dream you kill a snake shows you will overcome difficulties and enemies, and be successful in love, trade, or farming; but unsuccessful at sea.

SNOW: To dream you see the ground covered with snow, or that it is snowing, is a very favorable dream; to a young man, it shows he will shortly marry a virgin, who is very fond of him, and that he will have children by her, mostlygirls; to a young woman, it foretells she will marry a rich man, that he will have children by her who will become very affluent, and rise to honors in the state; to the farmer, it shows plentiful crops and increase of live stock; to the tradesman, it argues great increase of business; to the sailor, a pleasant and very lucrative voyage, and a rich sweetheart in a foreign port. If you are soliciting a place, this dream presages that you will obtain it; if you have lottery tickets they will be prizes; if you have a lawsuit you will gain it.

SOLDIERS: To see soldiers in your dream, shows troubles, persecutions, and lawsuits; to the lover they denote that the object of your affections will be obliged to quit their present place of residence by command of a father, on your account ; to the tradesman they presage loss of goods, and quarrels with creditors. To dream they are pursuing you, shows that you will be imprisoned and meet with heavy losses, and be much disliked by your rich neighbors. This is one of those dreams after which I would advise the party dreaming to change their quarters.

SPIT: To dream you are in a kitchen turning a spit is the forerunner of troubles and misfortunes; expect to be robbed, to lose your trade, to become very poor, and that your friends will desert you; if you are in love, it shews the object of your affections to be of a bad temper, lazy, doomed to poverty and misfortune.

SQUIRRELS: To dream of a squirrel, shows that enemies are endeavoring to slander your reputation; to the lover it shows your sweetheart is of a bad temper and much given to drinking, if you have a lawsuit, it will surely be decided against you; if you are in trade, sharpers will endeavor to defraud you, and you will quarrel with your principal creditor.

STARCHING: To dream you are starching of linen, shows you will be married to an industrious person, and that you will be successful in life, and save money; it also shows that you are about to receive a letter containing; some pleasant news.

NEW DREAM BOOK

STARS: To dream you see the stars shining very bright, augers success to the lover, and good news from a far distant country; to the farmer, they are the forerunner of a good crop, to the tradesman, great increase of business; to the sailor, a speedy marriage to a woman with money. If you dream, they are very dim, and are scarcely to be seen, then expect some heavy calamity, and many severe disappointments.

STRANGE PLACE: To dream of being in a strange place, denotes a good legacy from a relation whilst you are in prison; to the lover, they show inconstancy and want of affection in the object of our love; to the sailor, sickness on his next voyage.

SUN: To dream you see the sun shine, shows accumulation of riches, and enjoying posts of honor in the state; also success to the latter. To dream you see the sun rise, promises fidelity in your sweetheart, and good news from friends. To dream you see the sun set, shews infidelity in your sweetheart, and disagreeable news; tradesman loss of business. To dream you see the sun under a cloud, foretells many hardships and troubles are about to befall you, and that you will encounter some great danger.

SWALLOWS: To dream of these harbingers of spring is a very favorable omen; they denote success in trade, and riches to the dreamer; in love, they denote a speedy marriage with the object of your affections.

SWANS: To dream of seeing swans, denotes contention in the marriage state, many children, who will do well and become rich, and fill your old age with joy and happiness; to the lover they denote constancy and affection in your sweetheart; in trade they shew success, but much vexation from the disclosure of secrets.

NEW DREAM BOOK

SWIMMING: To dream you are swimming with your head above water, denotes great success in your undertakings, whether they, be love, trade, sea, or farming. To dream you are swimming with your head under water, shows that you will experience some great trouble, and hear some very unpleasant news from a person you thought dead; in trade, it shows loss of business, and that you will perhaps be imprisoned for debt; in love, it denotes disappointment.

TEMPESTS: To dream you are in a storm or tempest, shows that you will, after many difficulties, arrive at being very happy, that you will become rich and marry well. For a lover to dream of being in a tempest, denotes that you will have many rivals, who, after causing you a great deal of vexation, you will triumph over. It also foretells, that you will receive good news from a long absent friend, who will overcome many difficulties.

TOOTH: To dream you lose your tooth, denotes the loss of some friend by death, and that trouble and misfortune are about to attend you; to the lover, it shows the loss of your sweethearts' affections. To dream you cut a new tooth, denotes the birth of a child who will make a great figure in the world.

THUNDER AND LIGHTNING: To dream you hear thunder and see lightning, is a very good dream; it denotes success in trade, good crops to the farmer, and a speedy and happy marriage to the lover; if you are soliciting a place, you will obtain it; if you have a lawsuit it will go in your favor; it also indicates speedy news from a far distant country.

TOADS: To dream you see these venomous reptiles, augurs evil to the dreamer; they shew enemies and disappointment among friends; to the lover it denotes infidelity in your sweetheart, in trade loss by swindlers, and spoiling of goods. To dream you kill a toad, denotes that you will overcome an enemy, and discover a person who is robbing you, and in whom you place great confidence.

TOMBS: To dream of being among the tombs denotes a speedy marriage, great success in business and the gaining of a lawsuit; also the birth of children, and unexpected news.

TREASURE: To dream you find a treasure in the earth is very ominous; it shows that you will be betrayed by some one whom you make your besom friend; that your sweetheart is unfaithful. And grossly deceives you; if you should not be able to carry it away, then it denotes that you will have some very heavy loss; that if you have a lawsuit it will go against you by the treachery of your attorney; and that you will be waylaid by robbers who will ill treat you.

TREES: To dream you see trees in blossom denotes a happy marriage with the present object of your affections, and many children, who will do extremely well in life; to the tradesman, it denotes success in business; and to the sailor pleasant and lucrative voyages. To dream you are climbing trees, denotes, that you will make a fortune, and rise to honors and dignities in the state.

To dream you are cutting down trees, foretells heavy losses by trade, and by sea, and also the death of a near relation, or dear friend.

TURNIPS: To dream of being in a turnip field, or that you see this wholesome vegetable, denotes acquisition of riches and high employments in the state; to the lover they augur great fidelity, and an exceeding good temper in your sweetheart, and that if you marry you will be very happy, have fine children, and thrive in the world.

TRUMPET: To dream, you hear the sound of a trumpet, is a bad omen, and denotes troubles and misfortunes; to the tradesman, it presages the loss of business; to the farmer, bad crops; to the lover, insincerity in the object of your affections.

WALLS: To dream you are walking on crazy, old, and narrow walls, denotes that you will engage in some very dangerous enterprise, that will cause you much trouble and vexation; if you get down without hurting yourself, or the walls falling, then you will succeed; if the wall should fall whilst you are upon it, you will be disappointed; if you are walking between walls, and the passage is very narrow and difficult, you will be engaged in some quarrel, or other disagreeable affair from which it will require great circumspection and caution on your part to disengage yourself; but if you get from between them safe, you will, after some difficulties settle well in life, marry an agreeable partner, have children, and become rich and happy.

WALKING: To dream you are walking in a dirty muddy place, foretells sickness and vexation; to a lover, it denotes your sweetheart to be bad tempered and unfaithful; to the tradesman, it foretells dishonest servants, and loss of goods by fire.

WATER: To dream you are drinking water denotes great trouble and adversity; in trade, loss of business and being arrested; to the lover, it shows your sweetheart is fake, prefers another, and will never marry you.

WATER MILLS: To dream of being in a water mill, is a very favorable omen; to the tradesman, denotes great increase of business; to the farmer, abundant crops; in love, success, a rich sweetheart, and a happy marriage.

WEDDING: To dream of being married, or at a wedding, is a very unfavorable dream, especially for lovers, it denotes the death of some dear friend or relation, with loss of property, and severe disappointments.

WHEAT: To dream you see, or are walking in a field of wheat, is a very favorable omen, and denotes great prosperity and riches ; in love, it augurs a completion of your most sanguine wishes, and foretells much happiness with fine children when you marry; if you have a lawsuit you will gain it, and you will be successful in all your undertakings.

WOOD: To dream you are cutting or chopping of wood, shows that you will be happy in your family, and become rich and respectable in life. To dream you are carrying wood on your back, shows that you will rise to affluence by your industry, but that your partner will be of a bad temper, and your children undutiful. If you dream you are walking in an extensive wood, it denotes that you will quickly fall in love, and also that you will be often married.

WOOL: To dream you are buying or selling of wool, denotes prosperity and affluence by means of industry and trade; to the lover, it is a favorable omen, your sweetheart is thereby shown to be of an amiable disposition, very constant, and deeply in love with you. To dream of having wool on your head instead of hair, betokens a severe fit of illness, and unpleasant news from a far distant country.

WOUNDS: To dream you are wounded is a very favorable omen, especially if it be with a sword; to the lover, it denotes success in your life and with an agreeable partner, who will be faithful and affectionate; to the tradesman, profit and increase of business; to the farmer, an increase in his cattle and plentiful crops; to the sailor, a profitable voyage, with unexpected success in love.

WRENS: To dream of these pretty little birds, denotes great happiness and content through life; to the lover they are particularly favorable, they show your sweetheart to be of a kind and amiable temper, much attached to you, and one that will make you very happy in the marriage state.

Having now disposed, under general heads of the various interpretations of dreams, we wish to remark, that where ever we have made use of the word lover we mean it to apply equally to the male and female. We also flatter ourselves, that the explanations will be found sufficiently copious to answer the expectations of all our readers, who will find them in comparison far beyond anything of the kind ever yet published. Indeed, unless they were to pirate this work exactly they can never produce more than a mutilated and defective account of the science, because we are well assured, that the original manuscripts were never seen by any person in England, except the translators; we shall therefore conclude this article with advice how to obtain a clear and decisive information upon any particular dream which is as follows:

When you dream of anything of that you want to have then explained write the subject dream on a piece of fair paper, fold this paper in the form of a heart, get a gill of red wine, dip the paper in it, and leave it under your pillow; just as you are going to bed you must drink of the wine at three draughts.

By following this mode punctually, you will in your next dream have the full explanation of your former one. This mode also will enable the lover to dream of your sweetheart, by writing the name of him or her on a small piece of gilt paper, and observing the instructions above directed; mind the sir and christian names must be written at full length, also the age.

NAEVIOLOGY

Or the science of foretelling future events by moles

These little marks on the skin, though they appear to be the effect of chance or accident, and might easily pass the unthinking for things of no moment, are nevertheless of the utmost consequence, since from their color, situation, size and figure, may be accurately gathered the temper of, and the events that will happen the person bearing them, as our philosopher who was a most excellent anatomist, made these signs, from a very particular branch of his studies, the result of his great labors and long experience, will, we doubt not be found very agreeable to our readers, and we shall accordingly proceed to give them a faithful translation of his observations. To enable them to turn more easily to the definitions, we have arranged them under heads in the same manner as we have before observed in the expounding of dreams.

ON THE WRIST OR BETWEEN THAT AND THE FINGER TIPS: The person to be of an ingenious and industrious turn, faithful in his engagements, amorous and constant in his affections, rather of a saving disposition, with a great degree of sobriety and regularity in his dealings. It shows a comfortable acquisition of fortune, with a good partner and beautiful children, but some disagreeable circumstances will happen around the age of thirty, which will continue four or five years. In a man, it denotes being twice married; in a woman only once, but that she will survive her husband.

BETWEEN THE ELBOW AND WRIST: Shows a placid and cheerful disposition, industry, and a love of reading particularly books of science- it foretells ranch prosperity and happiness towards the middle of life, but after having undergone many hardships, if not imprisonment- it also denotes that your eldest son will rise to honors in the state, and marry a woman not of his own country which will bring him much riches.

NEAR EITHER ELBOW: Shows a restless and unsteady disposition, with a great love of traveling; much discontented in the married stale, and of an idle turn.No very great prosperity, rather of sinking than rising of condition, with many unpleasant adventures, much to your discredit. Marriage with a person who will make you unhappy, and children who will be disobedient, and cause you much trouble.

ON THE RIGHT OR LEFT ARM: Shows a courageous disposition, great fortitude, resolution, industry, and conjugal fidelity- it foretells that the person will fight many battles, and be successful in all; that you will be prosperous in your undertakings, obtain a decent competency, and live very happy. It denotes that a man will be a widower at forty, but in a woman it shows that she will be survived by her husband.

ON THE LEFT SHOULDER: Shows a person of a quarrelsome and unruly disposition, always inclined to dispute for trifles rather indolent, but much inclined to the pleasantries of love, and faithful to the conjugal vows. It denotes a life not much varied either with pleasures or misfortunes. They indicate many children, and moderate success in business, but dangers by sea.

ON THE RIGHT SHOULDER: Shows a person oi' a prudent and discreet temper, one possessed of much wisdom, given to great secrecy, very industrious, but not very amorous, yet faithful to the conjugal ties- it indicates great prosperity and advancement in life, a good partner, and many friends, with great profit from a journey to a distant country about the age of thirty five.

ON ANY PART FROM THE SHOULDER TO THE
LOINS: Shows an even and mild temper, given to sloth, and
rather cowardly, very amorous, but unfaithful; it denotes decay
in health and wealth, with troubles and difficulties in the decline
of life, and much vexation from children.

ON THE NETHER JAW: Shows a woman that she shall
lead her life in sorrow and pain of body which shall hinder her
from attaining and bearing of children If a man shall have the
form of a mole on his tongue, it demonstrates that he shall marry
with a rich and beautiful woman. If a man shall have a mole in a
manner behind the neck, it demonstrates that he shall be
beheaded except God through earnest prayer prevents the same.
If a woman shall have a mole on the throat, it signifies that she
shall marry both with a wealthy, and very fair, or comely man, it
also signifies she will have many children.

ON THE RIGHT THIGH: Shows the person to be of an
agreeable disposition, inclined to he amorous, and very
courageous. It also denotes success in life, accumulation of
riches by marriage, and many fine children, chiefly girls.

ON THE LEFT THIGH: Shows a good and benevolent
disposition, a great turn for industry. and little inclined to the
pleasures of love- it indicates many sorrows in life, great poverty
and unfaithful friends, and imprisonment by false swearing.

ON THE LEFT KNEE: Shows an hasty and passionate
disposition, extravagant and inconsiderate turn, with no great
inclination to industry and honesty, much given to the pleasures
of Venus, but possessed of much benevolence- it indicates good
success in undertakings, particularly in contracts, a rich
marriage, and an only child.

ON THE RIGHT KNEE: Shows an amiable temper, honest disposition, and a turn for amorous pleasures and industry. It foretells great success in love, and the choice of a conjugal partner, with few sorrows, many friends and dutiful children.

ON EITHER LEG: Shows a person of a thoughtless indolent disposition, of an amorous turn, and much given to extravagance and dissipation- it denotes many difficulties through life, but that you will surmount them all- it shows that imprisonment will happen to you at an early age, but that in general you will be more fortunate than otherwise; you will marry an agreeable person, who will survive you, by whom you will have four children, two of which will die young.

ON EITHER ANKLE: Shows an effeminate disposition, given to foppery in dress, and cowardice in a man, but in a woman it denotes courage, wit, and activity. They foretell success in life with an agreeable partner, accumulation of honors and riches, and much pleasure in the affairs of love.

ON EITHER FOOT: Shows a melancholy and inactive disposition, little inclined to the pleasures of love, given to reading and a sedentary life. They foretell sickness and unexpected misfortunes, with many sorrows and much trouble, an unhappy choice of partner for life, with disobedient and unfortunate children.

ON THE RIGHT SIDE OF THE FOREHEAD OR RIGHT TEMPLE: Shows an active and industrious disposition, much given to the sport of love. It denotes that the person will be very successful in life, marry an agreeable partner, and arrive at unexpected riches and honors, and have a son who will become a great man.

NEW DREAM BOOK

ON THE RIGHT EYE BROW: Shows a sprightly, active disposition, a great turn for gallantry, much courage, and great perseverance- it denotes wealth and success in love, war, and business; that you will marry an agreeable mate, live happy, have children, and die at an advanced old age at a distance from home.

ON THE LEFT EYE BROW, TEMPLE, OR SIDE OF FOREHEAD: Shows an indolent, peevish temper, a turn for debauchery and liquor, little inclined to amorous sports, and very cowardly- it foretells poverty, imprisonment, and disappointment in all your undertakings,with undutiful children and a bad tempered partner.

ON THE OUTSIDE CORNER OF EITHER EYE: Shows a sober, honest and steady disposition, much inclined to the pleasures of love- it foretells a violent death after a life considerably varied by pleasures and misfortunes- in general, it shows that poverty will keep at a distance.

ON EITHER CHEEK: shows an industrious, benevolent, and sober disposition, given to be grave and solemn, little inclined to amorous sports, but of a steady courage and unshaken fortitude. It denotes a moderate success in life, neither becoming rich nor falling into poverty- it also foretells an agreeable and industrious partner, with two children, who will do better than the parents.

ON THE CHIN: Shows an amiable and tranquil disposition, industrious, and much inclined to traveling and the joys of Venus- it denotes that the person will be highly successful in life, accumulating a large and splendid fortune, with many respectable and worthy friends, an agreeable conjugal partner, and fine children- but it also indicates losses by sea and in foreign countries.

NEW DREAM BOOK

ON EITHER LIP: Shows a delicate appetite, a sober disposition, and much given to the pleasures of love, of an industrious and benevolent turn- it denotes that the person will be successful in undertakings, particularly in love affairs- that jy will rise above your present condition, and be greatly respected and esteemed, that you will endeavor to obtain some situation, in which you will at first prove unsuccessful, but afterwards prevail.

ON THE NOSE: Shows a hasty and passionate disposition much given to amorous pleasures, faithful to engagements, candid, open, and sincere in friendship, courageous and honest, but very petulant, and rather given to drink- it denotes great success through life and in love affairs, that you will become rich, marry well, have fine children, and be much esteemed by your neighbors and acquaintances, that you will travel much, particularly by water.

ON THE THROAT: Shows a friendly and generous disposition, of a sober turn, given to industry, extremely amorous, and much inclined to indulge in the joys of Venus- it denotes riches by marriage,and great success afterwards in your undertakings, with fine children, who will go to a far distant country where they will marry, grow rich, and return to their native land.

ON THE SIDE OF THE NECK: Shows a meek and sober disposition, moderately inclined to the pleasures of love, but warm and steady in friendship, rather given to industry- it denotes much sickness, and that you will be in great danger of suffocation, bat that you will rise to unexpected honors and dignity, receive large legacies, and grow very rich- but also that your children will fall into poverty and disgrace.

ON THE RIGHT BREAST: Shows an intemperate and

indolent disposition, rather given to drink, strongly attached to the joys of love- it denotes much misfortunes in life, with a sudden reverse from riches to poverty- many unpleasant and disagreeable accidents, wit^ a sober and industrious partner; many children, mostly girls, who will marry well, and be a great comfort to your old age ; it warns you to beware of pretended friends who will harm you much.

ON THE LEFT BREAST: Shows an industrious and sober disposition, amorous and much given to walking; it denotes great success in life and in love, that you will accumulate riches, and have many children, mostly boys, who will make their fortunes by sea.

ON THE BOSOM: Shows a quarrelsome and unhappy temper, given to low debauchery, and exceedingly amorous, indolent and unsteady; it denotes a life neither very prosperous nor very miserable, but passed without many friends or much esteem.

UNDER THE BREAST OVER THE HEART: Shows a rambling, unsettled disposition, given to drinking, and little careful of your actions, very amorous, and much given to indulge indiscriminately in the pleasures of love, in a man. In a woman it indicates sincerity in love, industry and a strict regard for character; in life it denotes a mixture of good and bad fortune, the former rather prevailing; it denotes imprisonment for debt, but not of long duration; to a woman, it denotes easy labors and children who will become rich, live happy and respected, and marry well.

ON THE RIGHT SIDE NEAR THE RIBS: Shows an indolent cowardly disposition, given to excessive drinking, of an inferior capacity, and little inclined to the pleasures of love; it denotes an easy life rather of poverty than riches, little respected, a partner of an uneven and disagreeable temper, with undutiful children, who will fall into many difficulties.

ON THE BELLY: Shows an indolent slothful disposition, given to gluttony, very selfish, addicted to the pleasure of love and drink, negligent of dress and cowardly; it denotes small success in life, many crosses, some imprisonment, and traveling, with losses by sea, but it foretells that you will marry an agreeable partner of a sweet temper, have children who will be industrious and become very respectable in life.

ON THE PRIVY MEMBER OR PARTS: Shows a generous, open, and honest disposition, extremely disposed to gallantry and the joys of Venus, given to sobriety and of undaunted courage; it denotes great success in the latter part of life, but many and severe misfortunes in the former which will be borne with fortitude; it also foretells happy marriage and fine children who will be happy, thrive well, and grow rich and respectable; in man it shows that he will have natural children, who will cut a great figure in life, but he will experience much plague and vexation from their mother.

We shall remark to our readers, that it is of much importance to be particular in ascertaining the exact situation of the Moles, its form, whether it be round, angular or oblong; also its size and color, because these variations add or diminish the degree of those qualities and events which our authors' explanation has attached to each; for example, if the mole be perfectly round, then it denotes much good fortune, if of an angular form, a mixture of good and bad fortune, if oblong, then a moderate portion of good, a kind of happy medium; the deeper the color the more powerful will be either the good or bad fortune indicated; the lighter in color either will be in a less degree, as our author has uniformly spoken of a mediate color neither dark nor light; if it be very hairy, it denotes many misfortunes, but not so if only a few long hairs grow upon it, for then it shews prosperity in your undertakings; again, the larger the mole is, the more serious will be either the prosperity or adversity predicted; and the smaller it is, the less of either will fall to your share, our author has taken the middling size. Persons who wish to avail themselves fully of our authors' information, should not suffer an over-strained bashfulness to prevent their obtaining accurate information with respect to the situation, size, form and color; especially as in women a mole is frequently so situated in those recesses which modesty conceals from view, as not to admit of being discovered but by another; and yet to have a mole so placed is the most fortunate for them.

CHARTOLOGY

Or the science of foretelling events by card tossing

As many of those events about to happen may be easily, gathered from the cards, we have here affixed the definition which each card in the pack bears separately; by the combining of them the reader must judge for himself, observing the following direction, in laying them out:

First, the person whose fortune is to be told, if a man, must choose one of the four kings to represent himself- if a woman, she must select one of the queens, then the queen of the chosen king, or the king of the chosen queen will stand for the husband or wife, mistress or lover of the party whose fortune is to be told, and the knave o the suit for the most intimate person of their family; you must then shuffle and cut the cards well, and let the person whose fortune is to be ascertained, cut them three times, showing the bottom card- this must be repeated three times; then shuffle them again, let them be cut once and display them on rows on a table, taking care always to have an odd number in each row- nine is the right number- and to place your cards exactly under each other. After this consult the situation in which the person stands by the definition we have here annexed to each card, and after having repeated it three times, form your conclusion, remember that every thing is within your circle as far as you can count thirteen any way from the card that represents the person, his wife, or her husband, and their intimate friend; and also that the thirteenth card every way is of the greatest consequence; either the whole pack, or only the picquet cards may be used.

Another mode with the picquet cards is to shuffle and cut them, take three cards from the top; if there be two of a suit, take out the highest card, if three, take all; when you have gone through the pack, shuffle and cut the remainder, and do as before, and repeat the same a third time, then take a general view of all the cards withdrawn, and next couple them, a top and and a bottom card, then shuffle and cut them into three heaps, laying one apart in the first round to form a fourth heap- the first heap at the left hand relates to yourself entirely, the next to your family; the third is the confirmation of the former two- you must proceed a second and third time, adding each time one to the single card, and three single cards, given the connection of the operation; observe you must add the card which represents the person whose fortune is consulted to the three if it be not there already.

Ace of Clubs: Promises great wealth, much prosperity in life, and tranquility of mind.

King of Clubs: Announces a man who is humane, upright, affectionate, and faithful in all his engagements; he will be happy himself, and make every one with whom he has connection so if he can.

Queen of Clubs: Shows a tender, mild, and rather amorous disposition; one that will probably yield her maiden person to a generous lover before the matrimonial knot be tied; but that they will be happy, love each other, and be married.

Knave of Clubs: Shows a generous, sincere, and zealous friend, who will assert himself warmly for your interest and welfare.

Ten of clubs: Denotes great riches to come speedily from an unexpected quarter; but it also threatens that you will at the same time lose some very dear friend.

Nine of clubs: Shows that you will displease some of your friends by too steady an adherence so your own way of thinking; nor will your success in the undertaking reconcile them to you, or procure you your own approbation.

Eight of clubs: Shows the person to be covetous, and extremely fond of money; that he will obtain it, but that it will rather prove a torment than a comfort to him, as he will not make a proper use of it.

Seven of clubs: Promises the most brilliant fortune, and the most exquisite bliss that this world can afford; but beware of the opposite sex, from them alone you can experience misfortune.

Six of clubs: Shows you will engage in a very lucrative partnership, and that your children will behave well.

Five of clubs: Declares that you will shortly be married to a person who will mend your circumstances.

Four of clubs: Shows incontinence for the sake of money, and frequent change of object.

Three of Clubs: Shows that you will be three times married, and each time to a wealthy person. Too. This card will equally answer for a woman's being kept by three rich men according to her station.

Two of Clubs: Shows that there will be some unfortunate opposition to your favorite inclination, which will disturb you.

Ace of Diamonds: Shows a person who is fond of rural sports, a great builder, and a gardener; one who delights in planting and laying out groves, woods, shrubberies, and other such amusements; but that his enterprises of this nature will have success or disappointment according to the cards that are near it; it likewise signifies a letter.

King of Diamonds: Shows a man of a fiery temper, preserving his anger long, seeking for opportunities of revenge, and obstinate in his resolutions.

Queen of Diamonds: Signifies that the woman will not be a steady and industrious house-keeper; that she will be fond of company, be a coquette, and not over virtuous.

Knave of Diamonds: However nearly related, will look more at his own interest than yours; he will be tenacious of his own opinions and will fly off if contradicted.

Ten of Diamonds: Promise a country husband or wife with great wealth and many children; the card next to it will tell the number of the children; it also signifies a purse of gold.

Nine of Diamonds: Declares that the person will be of a roving disposition, never contented with his lot, and forever meeting with vexations and disappointments, and risks a shameful end.

Eight of Diamonds: Shows that the person in their youth will be an enemy to marriage, and thus run the risk of flying unmarried; but that if they do marry, it will be late in life, and then it will be with a person whose disposition is so ill assorted to theirs, that it will be the cause of misfortunes.

Seven of Diamonds: Shows that you will spend your happiest days in the country, where, if you remain, your happiness will be uninterrupted; but if you come to town, you will be tormented by the infidelity of your conjugal partner, and the squandering of your substance.

Six of Diamonds: Shows an early marriage and premature widowhood; but that your second marriage will probably make you worse off.

Five of Diamonds: Shows you a well assorted marriage with a mate, who will punctually perform the hymenial duties, and that you will have good children, who will keep you from grief.

Four of Diamonds: Shows the incontinence of the person you will be married to, and very great vexation to yourself, through the w hole course of your life.

Three of Diamonds: Shows that you will be engaged in quarrels, lawsuits, and domestic disagreements; your partner for life will be of a vixen and abusive temper, fail in the performance of nuptial duties, and make you unhappy.

Two of Diamonds: Shows that your heart will be engaged in love at an early period; that your parents will not approve your choice; and that if you marry without their consent, they will hardly forgive you.

Ace of Hearts: Signifies merry making, feasting and good humor; if the ace be attended by spades, it foretells quarreling in your cups, and ill temper to your family while you are in a state of intoxication; if by hearts it shows cordiality and affection between the parties; if by diamonds, your feast will be from home, perhaps in the country; if by clubs, the occasion of the meeting will be upon some bargain or agreement; if your ace of hearts is in the neighborhood of face cards of both sexes, with clubs near, it will be about a match making, if all the face cards are kings or knaves, or both, it will concern the buying or selling of some personal property, if all queens, it will regard conciliation between parties, and if queens and knaves, it will be about the reconciliation and reunion of a married couple.

King of Hearts: Shows a man of a fair complexion, of an easy and good natured disposition, but inclined to be hasty and passionate, and rash in his undertakings.

Queen of Hearts: Shows a woman of a very fair complexion or of great beauty, her temper rather fiery, verging on the terrible, one who will not make an obedient wife, nor one who will be very happy in her own reflections.

Knave of Hearts: Is a person of no particular sex, but always the dearest friend or nearest relation of the consulting party ever active and intruding, equally jealous of doing harm or good as the whim of the moment strikes, passionate and hard to be reconciled, but always generous and warm in the cause of the consulting party, though probably not according to their fancy, as they will be as industrious to prevent their schemes as to forward them, if they do not accord with his own disposition. You must pay great attention to the cards that stand next to the knave, as from them alone you can judge whether the person it represents will favor your inclination or not.

Ten of Hearts: Shows good nature, and many children; it is a corrective to the bad tidings of the cards, but may stand next to it; and if its neighboring cards are of good import, it ascertains and confirms their value.

Nine of Hearts: Promises wealth, grandeur, and high esteem; if cards that are unfavorable stand near it, you must look for disappointment and a reverse; if favorable cards follow these last at a small distance, expect to retrieve your losses, whether of peace or of goods.

Eight of Hearts: Points out a strong inclination to get intoxicated, this, accompanied with unfavorable cards, will be attended with loss of property, decay of health and falling off of friends; if by favorable cards, it indicates reformation and recovery from the bad consequences of the former.

Seven of Hearts: Shows the person to be of a fickle and unfaithful disposition, addicted to vice and incontinence and subject to the mean art of recrimination to excuse themselves, although without foundation.

Six of Hearts: Shows generous, open, and credulous disposition, easily imposed upon and ever the dupe of flatterers, but the good natured friend of the distressed. If this card comes before your king or queen you will be the dupe, if after, you will have the better.

Five of Hearts: Shows a wavering unsteady disposition, never attached to one object, and free from any violent passion or attachment.

Four of Hearts: Shows that the person will not be married till very late in life, and that this will probably proceed from too great a delicacy in making a choice.

Three of Hearts: Shows that your own imprudence will greatly contribute to your experiencing the ill will of others.

Two of Hearts: Shows that extraordinary success and good fortune will attend the person, though if unfavorable cards interfere, this will be a long time delayed.

Ace of Spades: Totally relates to the affairs of love, without specifying; whether lawful or unlawful.

King of Spades: Shows a man who is ambitious, and certainly successful at court, or with some great man who will have it in his power to advance him; but let him beware of reverse.

Queen of Spades: Shows a person that will be corrupted by the great of both sexes; if she is handsome, great attempts will be made on her virtue.

Knave of Spades: Shows a person who, although they have your welfare at heart, will be too indolent to pursue it with zeal, unless you take frequent opportunities of rousing their attention.

Ten of Spades: Is a card of bad import- it will in a great measure counteract the good effect of the other cards- but unless it be seconded by other unfortunate cards, its influence may be gotten over.

Nine of Spades: Is the worst card in the whole pack- It portends dangerous sickness, a total loss of fortune, cruel calamity and endless dissension in your family.

Eight of Spades: Shows that you will experience strong opposition from your friends, whom you imagine to be such- if this card come close to you, abandon your enterprise and adopt another plan.

Seven of Spades: Shows the loss of a most valuable friend, whose death will plunge you into very great distress.

Six of Spades: Announces a mediocrity of fortune; and very great uncertainty in your undertakings.

Five of Spades: Will pose very little interruption to your success- it promises you good luck in the choice of a companion for life, that you will meet with one very fond of you, and immoderately attached to the joys of Hymen, but shows your temper to be rather sullen.

Four of Spades: Shows speedy sickness, and that your friends will injure your fortune.

Three of Spades: Shows that you will be unfortunate in marriage, that your partner will be incontinent, and that you will be made unhappy.

Two of Spades: Always signifies a coffin, but whom it is for, must depend entirely on the other cards that are near it.

THE WHEEL OF FORTUNE
AND WHAT IS MEANT BY IT

When anyone desires to know a question, state any number not exceeding thirty. To that, let the number of the day be added and the first letter of your name which perhaps may prove a figure letter, and let the number be divided by three, and if the division comes out even, then expect a good issue of what you require whether relating to love, business, or the like. But if broken, and odd, then the success will be bad, if not altogether unfortunate.

SEVERAL QUESTIONS RESOLVING IN MATTERS OF LOVE AND BUSINESS BY THROWING A DIE, OR PRICKING AT A FIGURE, AFTER THE FORM AND RULES OF THE FOLLOWING TABLE

What number you throw, or what number or letter you prick upon, they being covered with a piece of paper, through which you must prick, go to the same number and letter in the following solutions for a true answer:

The Fortune Table

A 1 2 3 4 5 6
B 1 2 3 4 5 6
C 1 2 3 4 5 6
D 1 2 3 4 5 6

As to what kind of a husband a widow or maid shall have:

1: A Handsome youth be sure you'll have
Brown hair, high nose, he'll keep you brave

2: A man unto thy lot shall fall
Straight and neither short nor tall

3: An honest tradesman is thy lot
When he proffers slight him not

4: Fair, ruddy, bush hair is thy love
He'll keep thee well and call thee still his love

5: A widower though rich thou will marry
You for a husband won't long tarry

6: Proper and gay will be the man
That will thee wed my pretty Nan.

Whether a maid shall have him she loves:

1: Be not too coy he is your own
But through delay he may be gone

2: He of your wishes may be gone
He'd soon comply if it were so

3: Come set thy heart at rest I say
He will but plunder and away

4: Fear not thy neighbor is the man
And he will have thee if he can

5: Show him more kindness he will speak
His heart with silence else will break

6: Sigh thou no more he does relent
And his inconstancy repent

How many husbands you may expect, etc:

1: Come in the town thou first shall wed
A stranger next shall grace thy bed

2: With one well loved thy life shall be
And happy days in marriage see

3: The stars three husbands do presage
And thou shalt die in good old age

4: Wed thou betimes or else I fear
Thou wilt not much for wedlock care

5: Too much pride will make thee tarry
Yet after all that, thou shalt marry

6: Accept the ring thy love doth give
For long in wedlock he'll not live

Whether it be best to marry or not:

1: Don't fear, thy husband will be kind
And it is one shall please thy mind

2: If he be of complexion fair
For thee that man I do prepare

3: Come never fear it shall be well
Or say can no fortune tell

4: Pray lose no time for if you do
Age will come on and you may rue

5: If this match slip you may long stay
Then take the kind will without delay

6: Cupid commands thee now to do't
Then prithee make no more dispute

60659838R00057

Made in the USA
Columbia, SC
16 June 2019